Locked In But Not Locked Out

31-Day Devotional for the Incarcerated Soul

Albert J. Yancey III

Locked In But Not Locked Out
Copyright © 2025 by Albert J. Yancey III
Edited by Rhonda Bordes

Scripture quotations taken from the Amplified® Bible (AMP),
Copyright © 2015 by The Lockman Foundation. Used by permission. www.lockman.org. All rights reserved.

This book is intended to inspire, encourage, and challenge readers in their spiritual growth and faith journey. While every effort has been made to ensure scriptural accuracy, this publication is not a substitute for personal Bible study, prayer, or professional guidance when needed.
Printed in the United States of America.
ISBN: 979-8-90046-064-2
First Edition

For permissions or inquiries, contact:
Faith Beyond Incarceration (FBI) Ministry 501(c)3
Albert J Yancey III
P.O. Box 1041
Fresno, TX 77545
yancey.fbiministry@gmail.com

Dedication

To my Lord and Savior, Jesus Christ: Thank You for meeting me in the darkest places and never letting go. This devotional is dedicated to You, the One who sets captives free, heals the brokenhearted, and gives purpose to the forgotten. May every page reflect Your love, grace, and power to redeem even the most incarcerated soul. All glory belongs to You.

To my mother, Annette: My rock, my intercessor, my greatest supporter. You stood by me through every trial and tribulation, never wavering, never letting go. In my darkest hours, your love and prayers were a lifeline that reminded me I was never alone. This book reflects the strength and faith you poured into me, and I am forever grateful.

To my sister, Jodi: You were just 15 years old when my incarceration changed both of our lives. I know it wasn't easy growing up without your big brother by your side, and for that, my heart carries a quiet sorrow. But through it all, your love never wavered. Your support remained solid as a rock, even from a distance. I've watched you grow into a powerful, courageous woman, and I couldn't be prouder of who you are. Thank you for never giving up on me, for standing in the gap, and for reminding me that family love endures, even behind locked doors.

To my sisters, Merradean Pettit and Kymba Tullberg: Though life placed us on separate paths from birth, you were never absent from my heart. From as far back as I can remember, our mother spoke your names into my spirit, planting the seed of your existence deep within me. That seed grew into a love that time, distance, or circumstance could never erase.

To my Aunt Margaret: You have been a pillar of strength for our family, carrying burdens that would have crushed others. You've walked through unimaginable losses; burying your mother, father, two brothers, a sister, an aunt, a son, grandson, and so many others; yet you've remained steadfast. All while being a devoted wife, mother, grandmother, friend, advisor, and counselor to those who turn to you for comfort. You've done it all with grace, without a single complaint, and with a heart full of love. I want you to know how deeply I love you and how much I appreciate your belief in me. Your quiet strength and unwavering support have left a permanent mark on my heart.

To Mayor John Whitmire, Chaplain Thomas and Jennifer Lowe, Carl, and Bridgette Farris: Thank you from the depths of my heart for your boundless love, unwavering support, and steadfast belief in me. Your faith has been a guiding light, lifting me up and giving me strength when I needed it most. I am truly blessed to have you by my side.

To my family and friends: Thank you for your boundless love, unwavering support, and steadfast belief in me. There are not enough words or space to truly express how deeply each of you has been instrumental in my transformation. Having you in my life has been one of the greatest blessings; I am continually uplifted and inspired by your faith, kindness, and encouragement. Your presence has given me strength in the darkest moments and hope for a brighter future.

In memory of my Grandfather Albert J. Yancey Sr, Grandmother Essie Mae Davis, Father Albert J. Yancey Jr., Uncle Clarence O'Neil Yancey , my younger brother J.R. Yancey, Charles Fisher, Warren Ervin Sr., Pastor James Nash, and all family & friends who have passed on before this book became reality: You are always remembered and never forgotten. Though you are not here to see this moment, your love and spirit live on in every word. This book is a tribute to the foundation you helped build within me, and the strength you continue to inspire. Forever lives your legacy!

Foreword

By Johnny Chang

When I met Albert Yancey, I saw more than a writer, I saw a man carrying a vision through years of hardship. That vision was born in silence and confinement; the kind of silence that convinces people they are forgotten. Out of that place came these pages, not as theory but as a lifeline. Albert could not find a devotion that spoke to the reality of prison, so he began to write his own. For six years he carried that vision until it became what you now hold, a word that speaks with honesty, hope and power.

This book is more than a devotional; it is a testimony. It reaches not only the incarcerated, but anyone weighed down by unseen chains, and it points us to the gospel, the good news that Jesus bore our prison of sins opened the way to freedom and made us perfected and righteous forever by his sacrifice. To the one who feels confined or overlooked, may these words remind you of a greater truth. You may be confined, but in Christ you are never forgotten.

Acknowledgement

To God be all the glory! It is by His grace alone that I have the privilege to share this devotional, a journey of healing, faith, and freedom. This work is not solely the result of my experiences but also a reflection of countless hands, hearts, and voices that have supported me along the way.

Dr. Derrick Hunt: Thank you for playing an instrumental role in helping Faith Beyond Incarceration become a 501(c)(3) organization. Your diligence, guidance, and belief in this vision have laid a foundation that will impact generations.

Lewis Brazelton: Thank you for taking a chance on me and providing my first employment opportunity as an automotive salesman. Your trust helped me reintegrate into society with dignity and purpose.

Gene Cantwell and John Warner: Your wisdom, mentorship, and compassion have been a continual source of strength and clarity. Thank you for your unwavering presence and guidance throughout this journey.

Rhonda Bordes: my editor, thank you for lending your heart and expertise to this manuscript. Your thoughtful edits, gentle encouragement, and commitment to excellence shaped each page with clarity and compassion.

Damion Walker and Kevin Bruno: Your presence on the day of my release was divine. As you captured every step and word, you documented not just a moment of freedom but the reawakening of purpose.

Arthur Medina, Derek Hess, Sean Oliver, George "Doc" Houston, Dominique "Nick" Leonard, and Reggie McCoy: Thank you for being steadfast brothers. Your consistent support and heartfelt encouragement have profoundly impacted me. I am better because you walk beside me.

TDCJ Executive Director Bobby Lumpkin, Former TDCJ Executive Director Bryan Collier, Former TDCJ Director of Pardons and Paroles David Gutierrez, Texas Board of Pardons and Paroles Member Carmella Jones, and TDCJ Director of Chaplaincy and Volunteer Services Christopher Carter: Your leadership, support, and trust during the formative days of Faith Beyond Incarceration Ministry provided space for something sacred to grow. Thank you for recognizing the value of this ministry before it was fully realized.

To the churches and organizations; both within and beyond prison walls; that invested in me, prayed for me, equipped me, and never gave up on me: Your love is living proof that the body of Christ reaches even the darkest corners. Your contributions through Bible studies, worship services, care packages, reentry programs, and personal mentorship have profoundly shaped the man and the mission I walk in today. I carry your seeds of grace wherever I go.

To the board members and every volunteer of Faith Beyond Incarceration Ministry: Your behind-the-scenes dedication has been nothing short of remarkable. Whether organizing events, collecting hygiene items, crafting Mother's Day gift baskets, creating flyers, or traveling great distances; you are the lifeblood of this mission.

To my designer, Sayyam Shahzad & Rhonda Bordes: Thank you for sharing your creative gifts and vision. Your design brought this devotional to life, capturing not just the message but the very heart behind it.

To the men and women in correctional facilities who bravely shared their stories: Your honesty, pain, and hope poured inspiration onto every page of this devotional. Thank you for allowing me to walk alongside you, even if only in spirit and through Scripture.

Finally, to every reader, whether you are physically incarcerated or navigating a prison of the mind, heart, or soul; this book was written with you in mind. May these words remind you that no matter what your cell looks like, you are never locked out of God's love, mercy, and purpose.

With a grateful heart,
Albert J. Yancey III

Table Of Contents

Foreword V

Acknowledgement VII

Introduction XII

Good Morning Lord 1

Today – Act Like A Child 3

The Process 5

Polish Your Vision 9

Open Your Mouth 13

Deal With Your Demons 17

No Pain - No Gain 21

Forgiveness Sets You Free 25

Flirting With The Forbidden 29

Unwrap Yourself 33

There Was An Alternative 37

The Best Comes To Those Who Wait 41

Guard Your Testimony 43

Understand Your Inherited Position 47

Wrestling With The Enemy 51

Your Scars Matter 53

Do Not Disturb 57

I Don't Need Church 61

Work Unto The Lord 65

Dollar And Cents 69

The Betrayal Moment 71

Don't Take It Personal 73

Guarding Your Soul Against Agitation 75

Honor Thy Temple 79

It's Time To Unpack 83

Not Today, Please 87

From Time Into Eternity 91

Not Like Us 95

Close The Door 103

Good Night, Lord 107

About The Author 111

Locked In But Not Locked Out

Locked In But Not Locked Out

Introduction

Whether you are reading this behind concrete walls and steel doors or sitting in a world full of hidden battles, please know this devotional is written for you. I spent over 27 years in physical incarceration. I deeply understand the weight of confinement, the ache of silence, and the profound longing for hope. Yet, upon my release from prison, I discovered another type of captivity; one that doesn't rely on bars or barbed wire. Many appear free but are trapped by regret, addiction, trauma, shame, grief, or unforgiveness. Chains don't always rattle; sometimes they are silent; but no less real.

Inspired by my own journey through incarceration, this devotional is crafted specifically for anyone who has ever felt trapped. Within these pages, you'll find 31 days filled with scripture, reflection, honesty, truth, and prayer. I encourage you to engage with this devotional daily, beginning with Day 1 and progressing through Day 31. There is an intentional spiritual rhythm woven into these reflections; a journey intended to guide you from brokenness to breakthrough, hurt to healing, and confinement to clarity.

Once you've completed these readings, I encourage you to return to them whenever you face moments of struggle. Reread days that resonate deeply with your current circumstances and let the Word speak directly to your heart.

I am fully convinced that God never speaks to us exactly the same way twice. The Holy Spirit reveals fresh truths each time we approach with open hearts and willing spirits. This devotional is designed to continually speak into your life, bringing renewed strength for each new day, each fresh battle, and each tender wound.

Over these 31 days, we will journey together through themes of identity, forgiveness, purpose, healing, surrender, grief, and grace. We'll explore the lives of people in Scripture who experienced confinement yet were never forgotten; locked in, but never locked out of God's love, purpose, and plan.

My prayer is that just as God met me in my darkest moments, He will meet you through these pages; reminding you that you are neither alone nor without purpose.

Whether you're in a cell or a sanctuary, whether you wear state-issued boots or business suits, whether your chains are iron or emotional, always remember God sees you; God knows you, and God has not abandoned you.

Let me encourage you to have a pen and note pad handy as you venture through this devotional in your time along with God.

Read. Reflect. Return. Let God speak.

With humility and hope,

Albert J. Yancey III

Locked In But Not Locked Out

Day 1

Good Morning Lord

"Look at the birds of the air; they do not sow or reap or store away in barns, and yet your Heavenly Father feeds them." Matthew 6:26 (NIV)

As I stood by the window, my intention fixed on going to the gym, the gentle rays of the rising sun broke through the veil of darkness, illuminating the opposite window with a radiant glow. I squinted, captivated by the enchanting sight that greeted me; a symphony of birds gracefully maneuvering in the morning dew, their wings fluttering as they shielded their breakfast. In that tranquil moment, my mind traveled to the words spoken by Jesus in Matthew 6:26: "Look at the birds of the air; they do not sow or reap or store away in barns, and yet your Heavenly Father feeds them."

An immediate sense of conviction came over me as a gentle whisper from the Holy Spirit detained me in my thoughts. It became clear to me that amidst the rigidity of my life behind bars, I had grown accustomed to a programmed existence, my focus solely on my own schedule, appointments, meals, and trivial thoughts. Unintentionally, I had neglected to appreciate the gift of a new day bestowed upon me by God. In our incessant preoccupation with worldly concerns, we often overlook the subtle blessings He bestows upon us.

Many mornings, I skipped prayer to focus on my agenda or became frustrated by daily disruptions. However, as I allowed the Lord to touch the depths of my heart, I came face-to-face with the self-centeredness that had seeped into my relationship with God. This morning, a critical decision stood before me; to allow my personal aspirations to stifle God's presence in my life or to make Him the focal point at the start of each day.

It struck me how often we begin our day by acknowledging those around us, exchanging greetings of "Good morning" as we go about our daily rituals. Yet, we inadvertently disregard our acknowledgment of God. The way we start our day influences everything that comes after.

Who would have thought that watching birds receive their daily bread could so clearly highlight the importance of morning prayer? So, the next time you hear the saying, "The early bird gets the worm," consider reflecting on how you start your morning routine.

Reflection Questions:

1. How often do you begin your day with prayer or express gratitude for the blessings bestowed upon you by God?

2. What distractions or personal ambitions hinder your ability to prioritize God in the morning?

3. How can you foster a habit of acknowledging and seeking God's presence at the inception of each day?

4. Reflect upon the seemingly inconspicuous ways in which God has extended His grace and provision to you. How can you cultivate greater appreciation for these blessings?

5. Contemplate the potential impact of making God the primary focus of your day. How might such a shift in perspective transform your mindset and actions throughout the day?

Day 2

Today – Act Like A Child

"Let the little children come to me, and do not hinder them, for the kingdom of God belongs to such as these." Mark 10:14 (NIV)

As I sat in the sanctuary of our chapel, lovingly referred to as Emmanuel, I cherished the moments spent in the presence of God. It was my refuge, my Mount Zion, where I could escape the chaos of life and pour out my heart passionately to the Lord. In that sacred atmosphere. It was there I found solace and listened intently for the voice of God., little did I know that a profound message was about to be spoken to me: "Today - Act Like a Child."

When those words resonated within me, they struck like lightning, piercing through the darkness of my soul, "Lord, I am your child", I tenderly whispered in response, but the simplistic significance of those words began to unfold as I searched my heart and meditated on this revealed knowledge. God was highlighting a disconnection between us as He desired access to the deepest recesses of my heart; a place that had been guarded and inaccessible, even to God because of the pain, hurts and betrayals of the past.

Having experienced vulnerability in the past, only to have my trust mishandled, I became guarded and found it nearly impossible to let my defenses down. In doing so, however, I unintentionally kept God at a distance. There were wounds within me that He longed to touch and heal, yet I chose to endure the pain rather than embrace the release and freedom He offered.

Our Father in Heaven yearns for a deep relationship with His children, unfortunately, the hurts, disappointments, and pains inflicted by others cause us to inadvertently protect ourselves from potentially encountering those emotions again, even when it is God trying to reach us. God does not want limitations placed upon Him in reaction to the pain inflicted by others. He does not simply brush things aside the way we might quickly sweep dust under a rug.

3

Instead, He intentionally addresses each of our hurts, carefully sorting through the rubble of our experiences to bring genuine healing and restoration to our wounded souls.

If we truly desire to live the abundant life that God has promised, it is imperative that we remove the barriers that hinder Him from having full access to our hearts. Our Father will not force Himself upon us; rather, His love surpasses anything we have ever known or received; however, to experience His love, we must come to a place of complete dependency on Him.

This lesson is what Jesus wanted His disciples and all those who followed Him to understand when children were brought to Him. In Mark 10:14, Jesus declares, "Let the little children come to me, and do not hinder them, for the kingdom of God belongs to such as these." Have you ever wondered why Jesus, amidst the busyness of His ministry, chose to prioritize the children and likened them to the Kingdom of Heaven?

Children have a beautiful quality of innocence. They are willing to trust wholeheartedly and do whatever someone tells them. Think about the simple acts of childlike faith, jumping off a ledge into their parent's arms, believing in the existence of imaginary creatures, or fervently praying for the desires of their hearts. God desires for us is to embrace this same childlike mindset; one marked by unwavering faith and complete trust in Him.

As adults, many of us struggle to place our complete trust in anyone other than ourselves. It is common to hear someone describe themselves as "self-made" highlighting a sense of individuality and independence; however, this mindset hinders us from experiencing the fullness of God's love and grace, as He calls us to surrender our self-reliance and embrace childlike faith.

Reflection Questions:

1. How has past hurts and disappointments affected your ability to trust God completely?

2. In what ways can you cultivate childlike faith in your relationship with God?

3. What steps can you take to remove the barriers that restrict God from having full access to your heart?

Day 3

The Process

"For you have need of patient endurance [to bear up under difficult circumstances without compromising], so that when you have carried out the will of God, you may receive and enjoy to the full what is promised." Hebrews 10:36 (AMP)

In the story of the ten lepers who cried out to Jesus, we are given more than a miraculous healing account; we're invited to witness a lesson in obedience, process, and faith. These ten men approached Jesus with one desperate plea: to be healed. But rather than healing them on the spot, Jesus gave them a simple instruction: "Go, show yourselves to the priest." It was only as they went; as they obeyed; that healing began to manifest. This resonates deeply with my own walk of faith.

There's something sacred about the in-between; the space between prayer and promise, between surrender and fulfillment. In Hebrews 10:36, we're reminded that patient endurance is not just helpful; it's necessary. We must hold firm, even when answers seem delayed, knowing that the promise is not denied; only deferred until the process is complete. This resonates deeply with my own walk of faith.

I remember when I first began sincerely seeking God's help to break free from the habits and struggles that plagued me. I prayed with passion. I wanted instant change, and while there were moments of victory, there were also times I failed miserably. Triggers would arise, and I'd react in ways that contradicted the life I wanted to live. It felt like a daily war between who I was and who I knew I could be in Christ.

When I stumbled, instead of turning to God with repentance, I often turned inward. Shame. Condemnation. Isolation. Thoughts like "I can't do this anymore" crept in, and I questioned whether I was even worthy of God's plan for me. But I know I'm not the only one who's felt that way. If we're honest, many of us have faced that same discouragement; especially when we see others

5

advancing while we remain in waiting.

This is where the story of the people with leprosy becomes personal. They didn't see change at once. They had to walk in obedience even when they still looked and felt unclean. Sometimes, we want God to act with street speed; fast, now, on our terms. But God doesn't operate on our timetable. He works through Kairos, His perfect and appointed time. And His process isn't just about the destination; it's about the transformation that happens as we go.

We must ask ourselves: are we willing to walk even when we don't see the change yet? Can we trust God's instructions even when the outcome feels uncertain?

Too often, we focus on the unholy trinity; me, myself, and I; pouting when things don't go our way, doubting when prayers seem delayed. But Jesus is calling us to a higher mindset: one that trusts the process, even in the pain. Like the caterpillar undergoing metamorphosis, we can't skip the cocoon. Transformation takes time.

Today, I'm reminded that stumbling isn't failure; it's part of the process. When I fall, I will choose to repent, rise, and keep walking. God hasn't abandoned me. He is walking with me.

Reflection Questions:

1. How have you experienced struggles and failures in your Christian walk and how have these challenges affected your relationship with God and your sense of self-worth?

2. Can you recall instances when you prayed for a specific outcome but either heard nothing from God or did not see the desired result? How did you respond in those situations? Did doubt, frustration, or complaints arise? How can you shift your mindset and response when faced with unanswered prayers?

3. How has the desire for quick results and instant fulfillment affected your relationship with God? Have you ever tried to manipulate or rush God's timing? What lessons can you draw from this chapter to guide your approach to prayer and waiting on God?

4. Consider the imagery of the caterpillar undergoing metamorphosis. How does this resonate with your own transformation as a believer? What aspects of your old self (B.C. years) do you find challenging to let go of? How can you trust the process and embrace the changes God is working within you?

Day 4

Polish Your Vision

"Then the Lord answered me and said, 'Write the vision and engrave it plainly on tablets So that the one who reads it will run. For the vision is yet for the appointed [future] time; It hurries toward the goal [of fulfillment]; it will not fail. Even though it delays, wait [patiently] for it, Because it will certainly come; it will not delay."
Habakkuk 2:2-3 AMP

As I stated previously, I did 27 years in prison, but before my release, something unexpected happened. God planted a seed of purpose in my heart. That seed didn't come when everything was going well. It didn't come in comfort, stability, or freedom. It came in confinement. It came while I was still surrounded by walls, routines, restrictions, and the raw reality of incarceration. But in that unlikely place, God gave me a vision; a vision for a prison ministry that would bring light, hope, and healing to others who were walking the same dark path I had once walked. It was a holy interruption in the middle of a hopeless environment. And it lit something inside me that prison bars couldn't contain.

I had every reason to ignore that vision. I was still incarcerated. I didn't have resources, a platform, or even a release date in sight. To the natural eye, it looked like a dream that was too big for my situation. But God doesn't look at circumstances the way we do. He speaks to destiny, not limitations. So I decided not to wait until I was free to act on the vision. I focused on it. I prayed over it. And I wrote it down. Just like the Lord instructed Habakkuk, I made it plain; not just for myself, but for others who would come alongside me in the work. What started as ink on a page became a blueprint for hope.

And here's what still amazes me: others caught the vision. They read what I wrote and saw something bigger than me. They saw what God was doing. And

9

they started to run; not away from ministry, but toward it, carrying the message with passion, creativity, and faith. That's the power of divine vision. It doesn't stay with the person who receives it; it multiplies through those who are willing to run with it.

Even now, I'm watching this vision unfold in real time. Some parts have already come to pass. I've seen souls saved, lives transformed, and ministries birthed behind bars. Other parts are still developing; still being prayed through, worked on, or waiting on the right door to open. And yes, some pieces still feel far away.

But here's what I hold onto: God is faithful to finish what He starts. His Word reminds me that if the vision seems slow, it's only because it's moving toward its appointed time. And when that time comes, it will speak. It will prove itself to be true. It will not lie.

I've learned that God doesn't tease us with dreams just to disappoint us. He's not a man that He should lie. If He showed it to you, it's because He intends to bring it to pass. The key is not just to dream; but to wait in faith and walk in obedience while the dream matures.

So today, I encourage anyone reading this; especially those who are still incarcerated or in a waiting season; write the vision, make it plain, and don't despise your current condition or underestimate what God can do through you; even now. Whether you're behind walls or navigating life on the outside, your present does not cancel your purpose. If God gave you a vision, He would give you the grace to walk it out.

Don't let your environment dictate your expectation. God's vision will come to pass in His perfect time. You're not just surviving; you're becoming. And while you wait, keep building. Keep writing. Keep believing. Because the vision will surely come.

Reflection Questions:

1. What vision has God placed in your heart, even in difficult or unexpected places? (What has He asked you to carry and develop?)

2. Have you taken the step of writing it down and making it plain; for yourself and for others who may join you in it?

3. In what ways have you seen God begin to fulfill the vision already? Where are you still waiting?

4. What doubts, delays, or obstacles have challenged your faith in the

vision God gave you? How does Habakkuk 2:3 help you respond to those challenges?

5. Who has God placed in your life to help you carry out the vision? Are you allowing others to run with you?

6. Are you waiting passively for the vision to come to pass, or are you waiting actively walking in obedience, preparation, and prayer?

Locked In But Not Locked Out

Day 5

Open Your Mouth

Now Jesus was telling the disciples a parable to make the point that at all times they ought to pray ...." Luke 18:1 AMP

In today's fast-paced, technology-saturated world, genuine face-to-face communication is becoming increasingly rare. We text instead of talk, scroll instead of speak, and attend virtual meetings rather than engage in heartfelt conversation. These advancements have made life more convenient, but they have also created a subtle yet dangerous disconnect; not just from one another, but from God.

We can sit across from someone at dinner and never look up from our phones. And tragically, this silent disconnection carries over into our spiritual lives. Many believers have learned to outsource their communication with God; submitting prayer requests, attending group prayer calls, or asking others to intercede for them. While none of these practices are wrong in themselves, they were never meant to replace our personal prayer life.

Jesus said in Luke 18:1 that we "ought always to pray and not lose heart." He didn't say "sometimes." He didn't say "when it's convenient." He said always because prayer is the lifeline of the believer. It is how we connect with the One who holds all power, all wisdom, and all healing in His hands.

Let me be transparent: prison was one of the darkest seasons of my life, but it was there that I discovered the urgency and necessity of personal prayer. Prayer wasn't just a religious ritual; it was survival.

I couldn't depend on the chaplain to carry my soul. I couldn't wait for visiting ministers to lay hands on me. I had to open my mouth. I had to cry out. I had to become the intercessor for my own destiny.

As I reflect, I remember the example of my hot pot in prison. I took

13

meticulous care of it, emptying the water, wiping it down, maintaining it properly. But when someone else used it, they didn't handle it with the same care. Why? Because it didn't belong to them. And this is how it is with prayer. Your urgency will never be someone else's priority. What burdens you deeply may not move someone else at all. That's why you must open your own mouth.

We've been conditioned to stay silent before God; sometimes from shame, sometimes from pride, sometimes from fear. But silence can be deadly. The Nile crocodile has the strongest bite of any animal, yet you can keep its mouth shut with just two fingers or a piece of tape. Many believers are just like that: full of power, but silent. And the enemy knows; if he can keep your mouth closed, he can keep you defeated.

We cannot afford to lose heart in this hour. We must engage in fervent, persistent, personal prayer. Consider Hannah in 1 Samuel 1. She didn't just submit a prayer request; she poured out her soul before God. She didn't have polished words or perfect theology. She had a broken heart and an open mouth. And God heard her.

Let's stop comparing ourselves to seasoned intercessors or eloquent prayer warriors. God is not looking for poetic speeches; He's looking for surrendered hearts. Prayer isn't about performance; it's about connection. It's about refusing to lose heart, even when the answer hasn't come. It's about choosing to show up every day and talk to your Father.

Reflection Questions:

1. How has technology shaped your communication habits, with people and with God? Do you find it easier to scroll through social media and emails than to spend time in prayer?

2. What are some areas where you've outsourced your intimacy with God?

3. What deep struggles or hidden wounds have you been too afraid to bring before the Lord?

4. How might opening your mouth in honest prayer be the first step toward healing?

5. Do you believe you have authority as a child of God to speak to your circumstances in prayer? Are you exercising that authority, or allowing fear or shame to silence you?

6. What practical changes can you make to ensure that personal prayer

becomes a daily, non-negotiable priority in your life?

7. What would it look like to build a consistent rhythm of prayer in this season?

Day 6

Deal With Your Demons

"Through pride and presumption come nothing but strife..."
Proverbs 13:10 AMP

In the depths of our souls, there are often hidden forces at work; strongholds that quietly rob us of peace, purpose, and power. These are not always loud or obvious. In fact, many of us go through life unaware that a spiritual leech; a ruling demon; has attached itself to our inner man. Jesus addressed this reality when He was accused of casting out demons by Beelzebub, the chief of devils (Luke 11:15). Why would Jesus mention the chief unless there was an order; a hierarchy; among demonic spirits?

This truth became painfully real to me on the night of my arrest. Police officers burst into my home with guns drawn. I surrendered. I complied. I raised my hands and submitted to their authority. But though I surrendered outwardly, my past choices still carried consequences. My compliance didn't erase the crime.

That night became a spiritual parable for me. I realized later that spiritual surrender must go deeper than surface-level obedience. It's not enough to raise your hands in church or speak religious phrases. God is after your roots. True deliverance doesn't come from routines, rituals, or repeated declarations alone; it comes from confronting the ruling spirits behind your struggles.

Let's take anger, for example. Many cry out to God, "Deliver me from my anger!" But Proverbs 13:10 reveals the deeper issue: *"Through pride comes nothing but strife..."* That means anger is not the real problem; pride is. Pride is the chief ruler; anger is its weapon. If you cut off anger but leave pride intact, it's only a matter of time before anger resurfaces in another form.

The same goes for lust, addiction, manipulation, unforgiveness, and other

17

spiritual vices. We must ask the Holy Spirit to reveal the ruling spirit; the chief demon; behind the fruit we see. Otherwise, we'll spend years in cycles of temporary relief with no lasting change.

Jesus warned us in Luke 11:24–26 that when an unclean spirit leaves, it will try to return. If it finds your spiritual house "clean but empty," it brings back seven more wicked spirits; and your condition becomes worse than before. Why? Because the root wasn't addressed. The chief wasn't conquered.

Deliverance isn't a one-time shout; it's a lifestyle of examination, renunciation, and replacement. You don't just cast out; you fill in. You don't just sweep clean; you rebuild on truth. You don't just silence the symptoms; you slay the strongman (Luke 11:21–22).

The battle you're in is more dangerous than any war waged over land, power, or politics. It is a war over your soul; your thoughts, emotions, will, and imagination. And the enemy's goal is to keep the chief demon undetected so that the symptoms exhaust you and distract you from the source.
Let me say this plainly: If you are serious about being free, you must go beyond praying away what's visible and confront what's rooted. You must ask questions like:

- Where did this start?
- What opened the door?
- What lie am I still believing?
- What spirit is really driving this behavior?

Jesus did not come to manage our demons; He came to destroy the works of the devil (1 John 3:8). That includes the chief spirit that's been ruling areas of your life unchecked.

Here's the good news: You are not too bound to be free. When Jesus cast out the deaf and dumb spirit in Luke 11:14, the man spoke for the first time. That's what happens when the ruling demon is removed; you begin to function in areas that were previously locked down. God is calling you to that kind of freedom.

2 Timothy 2:21 (AMP) says: *"Therefore, if anyone cleanses himself from these things [which are dishonorable], he will be a vessel for honor, sanctified, useful to the Master, prepared for every good work."* If you let the Lord confront the root, you won't just be free; you'll be prepared and useful for His Kingdom. God doesn't just want you delivered; He wants you effective.

Reflection Questions:

1. What are the visible struggles in your life that may be symptoms of a deeper root? Ask God to reveal the chief spirit behind these patterns.

2. Have you unknowingly been treating your issues superficially instead of spiritually? What cycle of behavior or bondage keeps returning?

3. What does pride look like in your life? How has it contributed to strife, anger, or isolation?

4. What's stopping you from inviting God into the depths of your soul?

5. How would your life change if the strongman were removed? What would you finally be able to do, say, or become?

Day 7

No Pain - No Gain

"As for you, you meant evil against me, but God meant it for good in order to bring about this present outcome..." Genesis 50:20 AMP

Pain is a thread woven into the tapestry of life, one we would never choose, yet one that God often uses to prepare us for His divine purpose. In His sovereignty, what the enemy intends for evil, God masterfully repurposes for good.

Joseph's story, detailed in the book of Genesis, is a vivid reminder that God doesn't waste pain, He works through it. His journey didn't begin with power or prominence; it began with a dream. As a young man, God gave Joseph divine glimpses of greatness, a destiny that involved leadership and influence. But instead of being celebrated, his vision became the very thing that provoked hatred, betrayal, and suffering. His own brothers, those closest to him, threw him into a pit, sold him into slavery, and lied to their father about his fate.

And so it is with us. When God gives a promise, He often initiates a process. And the process almost always includes pain, pruning, and preparation. Like Joseph, we must be willing to endure the betrayal, the solitude, the false accusations, and the places where it feels like everything is falling apart. Why? Because in those places, God is forming the strength of character required to carry the weight of the promise.

In the pit, Joseph learned to lean not on his feelings but on his faith. In Potiphar's house, he learned stewardship. In prison, he developed humility, discipline, and a refined ear to hear God's voice, interpreting dreams with precision and compassion. Each painful chapter was not punishment, it was preparation.

God wasn't just elevating Joseph; He was building him into a man who could handle the responsibility of saving nations. And when the time was right, God

21

opened a door that no man could shut. Joseph went from prisoner to prime minister in a single day, but it took years of pressure, testing, and tears to prepare him for that moment.

That's why Genesis 50:20 is so powerful. When Joseph finally stood face-to-face with the very brothers who betrayed him, he didn't lash out. He didn't seek revenge. He looked back over his life and recognized the fingerprints of God in every dark season: "You meant evil against me, but God meant it for good…," Joseph could say this because he had come through the process. He endured the pain and emerged with perspective. What once felt like destruction, he now understood was divine construction. What others intended to break him, God used to build him.

If you've ever felt trapped, in your mind, in your heart, or in your circumstances, Joseph's story speaks directly to you. Seasons of confinement can drain your hope, stir deep frustration, and magnify sorrow. Yet even in those places, God is present. In His hands, limitations become lessons, tears become seeds of growth, and every setback becomes a setup for something greater. Trust Him in the waiting, because He is preparing you for the moment when your path opens wide to His purpose.

Like Joseph, you may have been falsely accused or grieve years you can never get back. But your current location does not cancel God's promise over your life. In fact, the depth of your pain may be a sign of the greatness of your purpose.

The process you're enduring is not wasted. Every lesson, every hardship, every tear is shaping something eternal within you. What if the delay is actually divine? What if the injustice is positioning you to one day speak life to others who are broken? What if the betrayal is birthing in you a spiritual maturity, endurance, and leadership you could not gain any other way?

Joseph didn't become who he was despite the pain, he became who he was because of it.

Reflection Questions:

1. What dreams or promises has God shown you that feel far from your current reality? Are you in a pit or prison season that makes you question those promises?

2. How have painful circumstances shaped or matured your character? Can you see areas where you've grown in wisdom, strength, or humility?

3. Are there people or events in your life that "meant it for evil"? How might God be repurposing those experiences for your good and His glory?

4. What would it look like to trust God in the middle of the process rather than just at the end?

5. What prayers or declarations can you begin making to stay aligned with God's purpose?

6. If God used Joseph's suffering to save many lives, how might He use your journey to impact others? Are you willing to let God use your story for the healing of someone else.

Locked In But Not Locked Out

Day 8

Forgiveness Sets You Free

"Bearing graciously with one another, and willingly forgiving each other if one has a cause for complaint against another; just as the Lord has forgiven you, so should you forgive.." Colossians 3:13 AMP

Forgiveness is not a suggestion in the Christian walk; it is a command rooted in Christ's example. In *Colossians 3:13*, the Apostle Paul urges us to "bear with each other and forgive one another... forgive as the Lord forgave you." These words call us into a higher realm of grace, where we do not wait for apologies or amends to extend mercy. Instead, we forgive because we've been forgiven, freely, fully, and undeservedly by God.

Forgiveness is not weakness; it is spiritual strength. It is not forgetting, it is releasing. When we choose to forgive, we unshackle ourselves from the invisible chains of bitterness, resentment, and emotional captivity. It is a sacred decision that unlocks peace, invites healing, and aligns us with the heart of God.

The life of Joseph is a stunning portrait of what it means to forgive as the Lord forgives. Betrayed by his brothers, sold into slavery, falsely accused, and imprisoned, Joseph had every human reason to hate. Yet, when the opportunity for revenge presented itself, he chose mercy. Why? Because Joseph saw with spiritual eyes. He understood what Paul later wrote: forgiveness isn't about the offender; it's about honoring God's redemptive plan.

Joseph said to his brothers, *"You intended to harm me, but God intended it for good..."* (Genesis 50:20). That is the heart of forgiveness, to trust that God is sovereign over our suffering, and that He will use even betrayal for His glory.

25

Unforgiveness is like drinking poison and expecting the other person to die. It festers and infects every area of our lives, spiritually, emotionally, mentally, and even physically. When we harbor unforgiveness, we take on a burden God never meant for us to carry.

Here's how unforgiveness silently destroys us:

Emotional Strain: Bitterness and resentment warp our ability to love, trust, and experience joy.

- Mental Health Struggles: Studies show unforgiveness increases anxiety, depression, and emotional instability.
- Physical Decline: Chronic stress from unresolved anger contributes to heart disease, high blood pressure, and immune dysfunction.
- Spiritual Disconnect: Jesus made it clear, if we do not forgive others, we block the flow of God's forgiveness and presence (Matthew 6:15).

What Forgiveness *Is Not*:

- Forgiveness does not condone the offense.
- It's not forgetting or pretending it didn't hurt.
- It's not about the other person being right, it's about you being free.

Forgiveness is a deliberate act of obedience to God that positions your heart to receive peace, clarity, and spiritual breakthrough.

- When we choose to obey Colossians 3:13 and forgive as Christ forgave us, the benefits are undeniable:
- Emotional Healing: Releasing the offense makes room for love, peace, and joy to return.
- Healthier Relationships: Forgiveness builds bridges where bitterness once built walls.
- Mental Relief: A forgiving heart is a light heart, free from cycles of rumination and inner conflict.
- Physical Health: Lower blood pressure, better sleep, and reduced stress levels often follow emotional release.
- Spiritual Renewal: When we forgive, we align our hearts with Christ and make room for His presence and power.

Steps to Walk in Forgiveness:

- **Acknowledge the Pain**
  Denial is not healing. Face the offense and the emotions it triggered.

- **Choose to Forgive**
  Forgiveness is not a feeling, it's a decision. You don't wait until you "feel like it." You do it in faith.

- **Pray for Strength**
  Ask the Holy Spirit to empower your decision. God's grace is available to help you do what feels impossible.

- **Practice Empathy**
  Seeing the humanity in your offender doesn't excuse them, but it can help you release them.

- **Let Go of the Debt**
  Trust God to handle justice. Forgiveness is trusting God's scales, not seeking revenge.

- **Embrace God's Greater Plan**
  Like Joseph, believe that even what was meant for evil can be used for good in God's hands.

Remember this truth: Forgiveness doesn't change the past; but it will transform your future. Like Joseph, your choice to forgive may be the very key that unlocks your destiny.

Reflection Questions:

1. Who do I need to forgive today? What am I still holding onto that God is asking me to release?

2. How has unforgiveness affected my emotional, mental, or physical well-being? What would healing look like if I truly let it go?

3. Do I believe that God can use the pain others caused for a greater purpose? How does Joseph's story challenge my perspective?

4. Have I ever received God's forgiveness without fully offering it to others? What keeps me from forgiving as Christ forgave me?

5. What would freedom feel like if I walked in total forgiveness? What relationships, dreams, or emotional weights might be restored?

Day 9

Flirting With The Forbidden

"Do not be deceived: God is not mocked [He will not allow Himself to be ridiculed, nor allow His precepts to be scornfully set aside]; for whatever a man sows, this and this only is what he will reap." Galatians 6:7 AMP

Temptation is not easily identifiable at the onset because of its subtlety. It disguises itself in justifications, feelings, and harmless indulgences. Yet what we often overlook is this: every choice we make is a seed. According to Galatians 6:7, we cannot plant seeds of the flesh and expect to harvest the fruit of the Spirit. The harvest of our lives will always reflect what was planted in secret.

The tragic story of Samson is a sobering illustration of this truth. As a man divinely set apart for greatness, Samson was empowered by God to be a deliverer of Israel. But over time, he began sowing seeds of compromise that ultimately reaped destruction. He didn't fall all at once, as his demise was a slow drift, a series of small, willful decisions that weakened his consecration, clouded his discernment, and caused him to forfeit his anointing.

In Judges 14, Samson's first recorded act of compromise was demanding a Philistine wife. Though his parents urged him to choose from among God's people, he refused. He said, "She pleases me well." That one decision revealed a heart more interested in pleasing self than pleasing God. We must ask ourselves: What seeds are we sowing when we prioritize pleasure over purpose?

As his story progresses, Samson kills a lion, then later returns to its carcass, scooping honey from its decaying body (Judges 14:8–9). As a Nazarite, he was forbidden to touch anything dead. Yet he not only touched it; he ate from it. This seemingly minor act was a major breach of his vow.

Sin often begins with small compromises we excuse it away by thinking:

"I can handle it."

"It's not that serious."
"No one will know."

But the law of sowing and reaping is unavoidable; every seed will produce a harvest.

By the time Delilah enters the story (Judges 16), Samson is already deeply entangled in compromise. Her manipulation only exposed what was already sown: a life lived too close to the edge of disobedience. Samson played with fire until it burned him.

He told her the truth of his strength, laid his head in her lap, and fell asleep, a picture of spiritual complacency. And when he awoke, he did not know that the Lord had departed from him (Judges 16:20). What a terrifying verse.

When we repeatedly yield to sin, our sensitivity to conviction gradually fades. We often fail to recognize when God's presence has departed because repeated compromise has seared our conscience. The consequences were devastating. Samson was captured, his eyes gouged out, and he was forced to grind grain like an ox; enslaved by the very enemies he was born to conquer.

Galatians 6:7 warns us clearly: Do not be deceived... whatever a man sows, that he will also reap. Samson's life teaches us that seeds of disobedience will always bear the fruit of loss, loss of strength, vision, and purpose.

Samson's story could have ended in shame; but grace met him in the prison. Humbled and broken, Samson prayed one final time, and God granted him strength to fulfill his calling. In his death, he destroyed more enemies than he had in his life.

This reveals a powerful truth: God's mercy can redeem a flawed harvest if we return to Him in humility. Though we may reap the consequences of our actions, God can still write a redemptive ending.

Today, examine your decisions through the lens of Galatians 6:7. What are you sowing? What you plant today will shape your spiritual condition tomorrow. Samson teaches us that strength is not found in outward power but in inner purity and obedience. Choose to sow to the Spirit and watch God produce a harvest of purpose, freedom, and victory.

Reflection Questions:

1. What seeds are you sowing in your daily decisions, obedience, or compromise?

2. Have you excused "small" sins, thinking they won't affect your spiritual strength?

3. Are there areas where you've ignored the Holy Spirit's warning signs?

4. What relationships or environments are drawing you closer to disobedience?

5. If your current decisions were to produce a harvest, what would that harvest look like?

Day 10

Unwrap Yourself

"Out came the man who had been dead, his hands and feet tightly wrapped in burial cloths (linen strips), and with a [burial] cloth wrapped around his face. Jesus said to them, "unwrap him and release him." John 11:44 AMP

In the depths of life's confinements—when hope feels out of reach and freedom seems like a distant dream—there remains a powerful and unshakable truth: Jesus Christ is still calling forth life. His voice cuts through the walls of fear, doubt, and pain, speaking directly to the hearts of the broken and bound. In John 11:44, we witness a moment of divine intervention that mirrors the inner struggles we often face when we feel trapped and powerless:

"The man who had died came out, his hands and feet bound with linen strips, and his face wrapped with a cloth. Jesus said to them, 'Unbind him, and let him go.'"

This verse captures more than a miracle; it reveals the process of resurrection and release. Lazarus, once dead, now stands alive, yet still bound by the very grave clothes that marked his past. He is alive, but not yet free. This is the condition of many who have encountered the saving power of Jesus: spiritually awakened but still wrapped in the remnants of who they used to be.

The grave clothes of Lazarus symbolize the emotional, mental, and spiritual bindings that remain even after salvation, guilt, shame, bitterness, pride, trauma, addiction, regret. These bindings may not be visible, but they restrict the soul just the same. And like Lazarus, many of us need to hear Christ's voice not only call us out of the tomb but command the next step: "Unbind him and let him go."

Jesus' words reveal a profound truth, resurrection is the beginning, not the end. Freedom is not only about coming alive; it's about being unwrapped, released, and empowered to walk fully in the newness of life. Christ doesn't just call us out of our tombs; He commands our release from everything that keeps us tethered to our past.

In the context of incarceration, this speaks volumes. The cell may restrain the body, but it does not have to imprison the spirit. Christ's call is to unwrap what remains, to deal with the hidden wounds and soul ties that still cling to us. And just like Lazarus, this process often requires others, spiritual community, godly counsel, and surrendered vulnerability.

Jesus did not personally remove the strips from Lazarus; He instructed others to do it. This shows us that healing often happens within community. Though Christ is the resurrection and the life, He invites others to participate in the work of deliverance. In our own lives, this can look like reaching out to a mentor, counselor, chaplain, or trusted friend. It may mean allowing God to use others to help us confront and release the things we'd rather keep hidden.

But there's something else here. Jesus didn't say, "Unbind him, and let him fix himself." He said, "Let him go." That's a command rooted in authority, compassion, and finality. When Jesus speaks freedom, it is not temporary, it is complete. The challenge for us is not whether Christ has the power to set us free, but whether we are willing to let go of the linen strips we've grown used to wearing.

There are times when we cling to grave clothes because they're familiar, because they feel like a part of us, or because we're afraid of who we'll be without them. But Christ's command is clear: let them go. Let go of what binds you. Let go of what reminds you of who you used to be. Let go of what keeps you spiritually stuck.

To be unbound is to walk in the light of new identity, renewed purpose, and resurrection power. Just as Lazarus stepped out of the tomb, you too can rise from the pit of despair into the fullness of life in Christ. This unbinding doesn't happen all at once, it is a daily process of surrender, confession, healing, and restoration.

Even when life feels confined, you are not locked out of freedom. The chains that matter most are not made of iron but of shame, pride, and sin—and Jesus has come to break them. His voice still echoes today: "Unbind him and let him go.

Reflection Questions:

1. In what areas of your life do you still feel bound, even after coming to faith in Christ? Are there "grave clothes" from your past that you have not yet released?

2. Consider: How have guilt, shame, or fear kept you from experiencing full freedom in Christ? What emotional or spiritual bindings might God be calling you to surrender?

Apply the necessary steps today to cooperate with Christ's command to "let go"! Who might God be calling you to forgive, confront, or invite into your healing journey?

Day 11

There Was An Alternative

For the wages of sin is death, but the free gift of God is eternal life in Christ Jesus our Lord. Romans 6:23 AMP

Life is full of choices; some bring blessing while others bring pain. Many of us know firsthand what it's like to make a decision that led to devastating consequences—a moment of anger, the influence of the wrong crowd, a desperate choice. But long before we faced outward consequences, many of us were already bound by the chains of sin.

Romans 6:23 tells us that sin pays a wage, and that wage is death, not just physical death, but spiritual death, separation from God, isolation from purpose and a life without direction, peace, or hope.

That is the path sin sets us on. And it doesn't happen all at once. Most of us didn't start off looking to destroy our lives or hurt others, we started with small compromises, ignoring God's warnings, and silencing His voice. He sent people, open doors, stirred our conscience, but we kept pushing forward, thinking we knew better. And yet, even after all that, God didn't give us what we deserved.

Instead of letting sin fully destroy us, He extended grace. We may feel like the consequences we received for our actions is an unbearable outcome, but truthfully, we could have been lost forever, separated from God with no chance of return. Thank God that in His mercy He interrupted our path.

Romans 6:23 gives us both a warning and a promise. Yes, the wages of sin is death, but it doesn't end there. The gift of God is eternal life in Christ Jesus. We earned the punishment, but He offered the pardon. We chose rebellion, but He offers relationship. Not because we deserve it, but because He loves us.

37

What if your captivity isn't the end, but the beginning of something new? What if this outcome is not your punishment, but your pause? What if, like Jonah in the belly of the fish or the prodigal son in the pigpen, this is your moment to wake up to the truth of God's love?

Your current situation may feel like the worst thing that's ever happened to you, but it might just be the space God is using to save your soul.

Let's be real, many of us were on a path toward destruction long before we were ever hit "rock bottom." But God, in His mercy, stepped in, knowing that sin would lead to death, and offered us another chance to turn our lives around and walk in a new direction.

He offers more than survival; He offers eternal life. Not just one day in heaven, but a new way of living right now. A life of peace, purpose, and power in the middle of difficult circumstances. That's the gift. It's not earned. It's not based on your performance. It's based on your acceptance of God's mercy and Jesus' sacrifice.

So the real question now isn't what you've done. it's what you'll do with this gift. Will you continue earning the wages of sin? Or will you receive the gift of eternal life through Christ?

You don't have to be perfect. You don't have to clean yourself up first. All you have to do is say yes. Surrender your life. Invite Jesus into the broken places. Let Him give you a new heart, a new mind, and a new future.

You may feel surrounded on every side, but you are never beyond the reach of God's grace.

Reflection Questions:

1. Looking back over your life, can you recognize moments when God was trying to warn or redirect you? How did you respond at the time?

2. Romans 6:23 says that the wages of sin is death. What kind of "death" (spiritual, emotional, relational) have you experienced as a result of past choices?

3. How does understanding God's gift of eternal life through Jesus change the way you view your current circumstances?

4. Are there areas of your life that you've kept from God, thinking He

couldn't redeem them? What would it look like to surrender those places to Him today?

5. How can you begin living in the new life God offers, even behind prison walls?

Locked In But Not Locked Out

Day 12

The Best Comes To Those Who Wait

"The Lord is good to those who wait [confidently] for Him, To those who seek Him [on the authority of God's word]." Lamentations 3:25 AMP

If there's one thing difficult seasons teach you, it's how to wait—waiting for meals, moments of rest, important news, visits from loved ones, changes in circumstances, answers to prayers, or even something as ordinary as waiting in traffic.

Time doesn't feel like time anymore; it feels like a pause. Everything is held in suspension. And if you're not careful, you'll start thinking that God is, too. That because you haven't seen the breakthrough yet, it won't come at all. That maybe He's passed over your name. That maybe the silence means forgetfulness.

But then Scripture whispers something different.
"The Lord is good to those who wait for Him..." This isn't passive waiting. It's not wasting time. It's waiting with confidence, waiting with the Word open and your heart expectant.

Lamentations 3:25 doesn't say God is good to those who hurry or who have everything figured out. It says He's good to those who wait, who lean in, who seek Him, who trust that even in the silence, He is working.

God does something in the waiting that He doesn't do in the rushing. He slows you down to shape you up. He lets silence teach you what noise never could.

Remember Joseph? He was wrongly accused and confined for a crime he didn't commit. While the world overlooked him, God was shaping and preparing him. When the moment arrived, Joseph wasn't just freed—he was fully ready.

Think about David. He was anointed by the prophet Samuel to be king when he was still a young shepherd boy, but he had to wait about 15 years before he actually became king of all Israel.

And think about Jesus, waiting 30 years before He ever preached a sermon. Thirty silent years of obedience, character, and preparation for a three-year ministry that would change the world.

Lamentations 3:25 doesn't promise a quick fix. It promises God Himself. He is good *to* those who wait, but more than that, He is the goodness you receive in the waiting.

Sometimes the miracle isn't what you get when the wait is over.
Sometimes the miracle is who you become while you wait, so while you wait, worship; don't wait idly, wait intentionally.

Serve someone else, become the answer to someone else's prayer, seek Him in the Word, and feed your spirit with truth. Stay honest with Him, bring your doubts, your fears, and your longing and cast them at his feet; He can handle it.

God sees the tears no one else sees, He hears the prayers you whisper at night, He's not late and He's not finished yet. This wait has purpose. This silence is filled with strategy, as you are being prepared for what you cannot yet see. Let today be a day of renewed trust.

Reflection Questions:

1. What are you waiting on God for right now? Be honest. Be specific.

2. In your waiting, are you drawing closer to God, or drifting away?

3. What is one way God has already used this waiting season to grow you?

4. Read Lamentations 3:25 again. What does it mean to you personally today?

5. What small act of faith can you take today to wait well, worship, serve, pray, study, or encourage?

Day 13

Guard Your Testimony

"And show your own self in all respects to be a pattern and model of good deeds and works, teaching what is unadulterated; showing gravity [having the strictest regard for truth and purity of motive], with dignity and seriousness. And let your instruction be sound and fit and wise and wholesome, vigorous, and irrefutable and above censure, so that the opponent may be put to shame, finding nothing discrediting or evil to say about us" Titus 2:7–8 AMPC

There is something powerful about your story—not just the challenges you've faced or the seasons you've endured, but how God has brought you through it all. Your testimony isn't just a chapter from your past; it's a weapon in your present and a beacon of hope for someone else's future. But like any precious gift, that testimony must be guarded. That light must be preserved.

When you surrendered your life to Christ, you became a living, breathing witness of His transforming power. And whether you realize it or not, people are watching you. They're observing how you walk, how you speak, how you respond under pressure, and whether your faith holds steady when life gets hard. That's why it's essential to guard your testimony. It's not about appearing perfect; it's about being real and consistent, even when no one's around.

Your testimony is more than just a single story shared once. It goes beyond the moment you first reached out to God. It's the ongoing proof of His faithfulness through every high and every low. It's what people notice when you're under pressure. It's how you treat others when no one is watching. It's choosing to do what's right even when it's easier to do wrong. In a world filled with challenges and discouragement, your testimony can shine as a powerful beacon of hope.

Scripture warns us that the enemy is always seeking to destroy what God has done in us. His goal isn't just to drag you back into old habits; he wants to discredit your story. If he can provoke you to lash out in anger, gossip, disrespect authority, or compromise your integrity, he'll attempt to make your faith look like fraud. First Peter 5:8 (AMPC) reminds us, "Be well balanced (temperate, sober of mind), be vigilant and cautious at all times; for that enemy of yours, the devil, roams around like a lion roaring [in fierce hunger], seeking someone to seize upon and devour."

Sometimes, that devouring doesn't come through catastrophe; it comes through carelessness. One argument. One reckless word. One lapse in judgment. That's all it takes to taint your influence. The Apostle Paul urged Titus, "And show your own self in all respects to be a pattern and model of good deeds and works, teaching what is unadulterated, showing gravity [having the strictest regard for truth and purity of motive], with dignity and seriousness. And let your instruction be sound and fit and wise and wholesome, vigorous, and irrefutable and above censure, so that the opponent may be put to shame, finding nothing discrediting or evil to say about us" Titus 2:7–8, AMPC.

You don't need a microphone or a platform to lead. What God is looking for is consistency; faithful character, quiet strength, and a life that reflects Christ. You've come too far to turn back now. You've been through too much to start acting like the person you used to be. Your journey is sacred. Your growth is real. Your testimony is a treasure; guard it.

Guard your heart because everything you do flows from it. Watch your speech, your motives, your responses, and your associations; not to impress people, but because you represent Christ. Your life is preaching, even when your mouth is silent.

There's someone near you right now who is hurting. Someone who's ready to give up. And they're watching you; not for perfection, but for proof. When they see you hold your peace under pressure, love the unlovable, and walk with integrity when it would be easier not to, something shifts in them. They begin to believe that change is possible.

Let your walk stir up curiosity. Let your peace raise questions. Let your joy baffle those who know what you've been through. And when the opportunity comes, don't hesitate to say, "It's not me; it's God. He changed my life. And He can change yours, too."

Reflection Questions:

1. Are you guarding your testimony, or have you been careless with your witness?

2. What areas of your life need to be strengthened so your actions reflect your faith?

3. Who around you may be silently watching your example for hope?

4. How can your story today be used to encourage someone else's tomorrow?

Day 14

Understand Your Inherited Position

"The Spirit himself testifies with our spirit that we are God's children. Now if we are children, then we are heirs—heirs of God and co-heirs with Christ..."
Romans 8:16–17 (AMPC)

There is a truth that has the power to radically transform your entire life once you genuinely embrace it in your heart: You are no longer who the world labeled you to be; you are exactly who God declares you to be.

When you surrendered your life to Christ, something extraordinary happened. You didn't just take on a new set of beliefs; you became part of a royal family. You were adopted by the King of Kings, receiving a position, identity, and destiny that no circumstance can take away. Take a moment to let this truth sink deeply into your soul. God does not see you by your past mistakes or current struggles. Though life may feel confining at times, you are not defined by what you've been through. Through Christ, your identity has transformed—you are now a beloved child of God. Your place in His family is secure, not earned but graciously given the moment you accepted Jesus.

The Apostle Paul explains this beautifully in Galatians 4:7, "So you are no longer a slave, but God's child; and since you are his child, God has made you also an heir." An heir doesn't have to struggle to claim their inheritance; it is already theirs by virtue of their lineage. Your inheritance goes far beyond earthly possessions; it encompasses peace, divine authority, purpose, eternal salvation, and everlasting life.

Yet, you may still wonder, "If I'm God's child, why am I facing so many difficulties? Why am I still imprisoned, still lonely, still hurting?" Consider Joseph's life story from the book of Genesis. Though divinely favored and

47

chosen, Joseph endured betrayal, slavery, and prison. Yet none of these hardships altered his status as God's chosen one. When God's appointed time arrived; Joseph's "due season;" he was exalted and positioned exactly as God had purposed.

Understand that the enemy seeks to erase your identity, entangling you in shame, guilt, and regret. But when you fully grasp your position in Christ, you cease striving for approval; you begin confidently walking in your true identity. Being God's child means unrestricted access to your Heavenly Father, access to His throne, His promises, and His unconditional love. Hebrews 4:16 affirms, "Let us then approach God's throne of grace with confidence, so that we may receive mercy and find grace to help us in our time of need."
You are not a beggar or an outsider; you are a rightful heir. You may feel wounded or discouraged, but your birthright as God's child remains intact. Refuse to settle for less than what God has prepared for you.
The enemy whispers deceitful words to hold you back:

- "You'll always be a criminal."
- "You're too damaged for God."
- "Your past disqualifies you."

But Scripture declares otherwise in 2 Corinthians 5:17: "If anyone is in Christ, the new creation has come: The old has gone, the new is here!" While your record on earth may display one story, Heaven records another; that you are redeemed, reconciled, and restored.

Recognizing your true position in Christ will change the way you live. You'll pray boldly, forgive quickly, resist temptation confidently, and no longer seek validation from others, knowing that you already have your Father's complete approval.

Life's challenges do not pause your inheritance or delay God's divine plan. Even now, He is shaping, strengthening, and setting you apart.
Start living as a son or daughter who carries Heaven's DNA:

- Speak life.
- Choose righteousness.
- Reject lies.
- Embrace grace.

Remember, your divine position isn't something you earn; it is your inheritance.

Reflection Questions:

1. Do you truly believe you are God's child; fully loved, accepted, and chosen?

2. In what ways has the enemy tried to bind you to your past? What lies do you still wrestle with?

3. Identify practical steps you can take daily to embrace and live out your identity as a child of

4. How does knowing your identity in Christ affect your relationships, your attitude, and your responses to adversity?

5. What specific promises from Scripture can you memorize and declare to reaffirm your true identity?

6. How might fully accepting your position in God's family change the way you approach your current circumstances?

7. What areas of your life require deeper surrender to fully experience your inheritance as God's child?

Day 15

Wrestling With The Enemy

"For we are not wrestling with flesh and blood [contending only with physical opponents], but against the despotisms, against the powers, against [the master spirits who are] the world rulers of this present darkness, against the spirit forces of wickedness in the heavenly (supernatural) sphere." Ephesians 6:12 (AMPC)

Every morning, whether you realize it or not, a bell rings in the spiritual realm announcing another round in a battle you did not choose but cannot escape. You may feel trapped by circumstances, but your fiercest fight is not with the outside world. The real war is being waged in your thoughts, in your spirit, and over your identity as a child of God.

Paul calls this a wrestle. It is not distant warfare; it is face-to-face combat. The enemy is not far away. He leans in close, whispering accusations, planting lies, and tempting you to believe that your failures define you. He is relentless in trying to drag you back into guilt, shame, and spiritual paralysis. And his greatest weapon is deception. If he can convince you that your struggle is only with people, systems, or the visible world around you, he remains hidden while you exhaust yourself fighting shadows.

The moment you realize the true nature of the battle, everything shifts. You stop misdirecting your energy toward people or circumstances and start resisting the enemy in the power of God. You begin to see that most battles first take root in the mind. The enemy whispers, "You'll never change. God has forgotten you. You'll always be who you were. Why even try?" Lies like this grow into chains heavier than any shackle. But Scripture commands us to take every thought captive and make it obedient to Christ (2 Corinthians 10:5). You are not a prisoner to every idea that enters your mind. If it does not align with God's truth, cast it out.

God does not send His children into battle unarmed. Through His Spirit and

His Word, He equips us with armor that is essential for victory (Ephesians 6:13–18). The belt of truth holds everything together when lies try to unravel you. The breastplate of righteousness guards your heart with the assurance that your standing with God is based on Christ, not your performance. The shoes of the gospel anchor your steps in peace, no matter the chaos around you. The shield of faith extinguishes every flaming arrow of accusation and fear. The helmet of salvation secures your mind in the unshakable reality that you belong to God. And the sword of the Spirit, the Word of God, is your weapon to strike back, declaring the truth like Jesus did in the wilderness: "It is written."

Worship, too, is a weapon. It shifts atmospheres. It confuses the enemy and breaks chains in ways human effort cannot. Paul and Silas sang in a prison cell at midnight, and doors opened while chains fell (Acts 16). When you lift God high, even when your circumstances remain low, you remind the enemy that the battle has already been won. At the cross, Jesus disarmed every power and principality, making a public spectacle of them (Colossians 2:15). You are not striving for victory; you are enforcing a victory already secured by Christ.

Every day is another round, but you are not without power. Begin each morning by thanking God for His strength and declaring one promise aloud. Midday, pause to examine your thoughts, are you believing God's truth or the enemy's lies? At night, reflect and thank Him for His grace, even where you fell short. Write scriptures down, carry them with you, and speak to them aloud until they become your default response when the enemy strikes.

You are not fighting for your freedom; you are fighting from a freedom Christ already purchased. Walk into each day aware, armored, and unafraid. The enemy may wrestle you, but he cannot defeat the one who stands clothed in Christ and rooted in truth.

Reflection Questions:

1. What recurring thought or lie has been trying to pin you down?

2. What scripture can you speak today to confront and replace that lie?

3. Which piece of God's armor do you most need to strengthen in your life right now, and why?

4. How can you intentionally worship this week, regardless of your circumstances, as an act of warfare and trust?

Day 16

Your Scars Matter

"And they have overcome (conquered) him by means of the blood of the Lamb and by the utterance of their testimony, for they did not love and cling to life even when faced with death [holding their lives cheap till they had to die for their witnessing]."
Revelation 12:11 (AMPC)

We all carry scars. Some can be seen on our skin, but others run deep in our hearts and souls; marks from wounds that no one else can see, memories of failures, betrayals, losses, and battles we thought might break us. For many, those scars feel like shame, a reminder of everything we wish we could erase. But in God's hands, scars don't signal defeat, they proclaim victory.

Scars tell a story. They are not just remnants of what hurt us; they are evidence of what we survived, proof of the healing we have received, and signs that God's grace was greater than our pain. Yet, so often, we try to hide them. We fear what people will think. We let the enemy whisper that our story disqualifies us from being used by God. But Revelation 12:11 tells us the opposite. It declares that our victory is not found in pretending we were never wounded, but in testifying to how God brought us through, combined with the blood of the Lamb that sealed our redemption.

The enemy thrives on silence. He would rather you bury your story than share it. He wants your scars to remain hidden so others can stay bound in shame, thinking no one else could possibly understand their struggle. But the moment you speak, when you tell someone that God met you in your darkest pit, that His mercy pulled you out, that His power carried you through, you deal a blow to the accuser. Your testimony becomes a weapon, a sword of hope for someone else's battle.

Even Jesus chose to keep His scars. After His resurrection, He could have returned with a flawless, glorified body, but He didn't. When Thomas

53

doubted, Jesus held out His hands and side, inviting him to touch the very marks of His suffering. Those scars weren't a sign of weakness; they were proof of His victory over death. They turned doubt into belief. In the same way, the scars you bear, whether from addiction, abuse, rejection, loss, or sin, are not to be erased or hidden. They are evidence that death, defeat, and despair didn't win. They point to the God who heals, redeems, and restores.

Paul understood this truth when he wrote, "But He said to me, My grace (My favor and loving-kindness and mercy) is enough for you [sufficient against any danger and enables you to bear the trouble manfully]; for My strength and power are made perfect (fulfilled and completed) and show themselves most effective in [your] weakness. Therefore, I will all the more gladly glory in my weaknesses and infirmities, that the strength and power of Christ (the Messiah) may rest (yes, may pitch a tent over and dwell) upon me!" (2 Corinthians 12:9, AMPC). Paul didn't boast about his accomplishments; he boasted about his struggles because they became the stage for God's strength.

There are people right now wrestling with hopelessness, shame, fear, and bondage, silently believing no one could ever understand or that their brokenness is beyond repair. Your testimony can break that lie. When you speak about what God has done, how He met you in your worst moment and rewrote your story, you give others the courage to believe that He can do the same for them.

Peter's life is a testimony to this. He denied Jesus three times, crushed by failure and shame. Yet, when Jesus restored him, Peter became one of the boldest voices for the Gospel. His greatest failure became the very backdrop for God's redeeming power. What Peter could have kept buried became the very story God used to strengthen the church.

Your scars are not a curse. They are not evidence of where you lost, they are evidence of where God won. They are reminders that you are still here because His grace is still working. When you share your testimony, you aren't glorifying your past; you're magnifying His mercy. You are declaring that the same blood that washed you clean can wash someone else, and the same God who lifted you up will lift them too.

Reflection Questions:

1. Are you still hiding parts of your past out of shame or fear? Have you asked God to help you release that shame, remembering that in Christ you are a new creation (2 Corinthians 5:17 AMPC)?

2. Are you willing to share your story; whether in simple conversations or openly; to testify of what God has done in your life? Who might

need to hear it today?

3. When you share your testimony, do you point to Christ as the source of your transformation? How can you ensure He receives the glory, not you?

4. Who around you is walking through something you've already overcome? How can you intentionally encourage them and remind them that God is still authoring their story?

Day 17

Do Not Disturb

"He who willfully separates and estranges himself [from God and man] seeks his own desire and pretext to break out against all wise and sound judgment."
Proverbs 18:1 (AMPC)

There are moments when it feels almost natural to pull back, to withdraw from people, to shut the door on connection and hang a silent "Do Not Disturb" sign over your heart. You wear your silence like armor and your glare like a shield, not because you want to be rude or rebellious, but because something deep within feels too fragile to face the world. Exhaustion sets in, frustrations mount, and invisible storms rage inside, leaving you retreating into yourself just to breathe.

Isolation can feel like safety. It can feel like control. You convince yourself that pulling away will keep you from more pain, from more expectations, from more questions you don't know how to answer. But walls built to protect can quickly turn into prisons. And some of us have become experts at emotional lockdown; not chained by steel bars, but bound by the invisible weight of trauma, regret, shame, or pride.

We tell ourselves that solitude is easier, but isolation is rarely neutral. In the quiet, our thoughts can twist. The enemy loves silence because it amplifies his lies: *No one cares. You're better off alone. Even God has left you.* The longer we retreat, the more these whispers start to sound like truth. But they're not truth; they're traps. God has not left you, and not everyone is against you. What feels like abandonment is often the enemy's attempt to keep you from the very connections and healing God has for you.

Even Jesus did not walk His path alone. The Son of God surrounded Himself with disciples. He ate with them, wept with them, prayed with them, taught them, and even leaned on them in His most sorrowful moments. If Jesus, perfect and divine, chose not to carry His burdens in isolation, why do we think we can?

When we wall ourselves off, we not only keep others from helping us; we cut ourselves off from the wisdom, comfort, and correction that God often sends through people. Proverbs 18:1 warns that those who isolate themselves "break out against all wise and sound judgment." Think about how many of your worst choices came when you were determined to shut everyone out, convinced that no one could tell you anything? Isolation has a way of turning pain into bitterness and pride into rebellion, making it nearly impossible to hear God clearly or receive guidance from those who genuinely care.
The danger is that, over time, we not only withdraw from people, but our hearts begin to close off to God. We may still speak prayers with our lips, but our hearts grow distant. We start talking *at* Him rather than *to* Him. We lose intimacy, peace, and direction, not because God has turned away, but because we've shut the door from the inside.

But God is patient. He will not kick down the door, but He will knock. He will speak through the tug in your spirit, through the kindness of someone who notices you, through words on a page like these. Maybe this is His knock right now; His way of saying, "Come out of hiding. I see the weariness. I know the weight. Let Me in. I want to walk this with you."

You may believe no one understands the depth of your struggle. Yet, if you look around, you're not the only one quietly fighting despair, grief, or confusion. Someone near you is wrestling too; the man in the bunk beside you, the woman serving chow, the person you see pacing the yard. What if your willingness to open up; to God and even to one person; is not just for your healing, but for theirs as well?

True strength is not in pretending you're fine. It's in admitting when you're not and still choosing to seek God anyway. It's in saying, "Lord, I'm broken, but I'm still here. I'm still listening. I still believe You can heal me." That kind of honesty becomes the doorway to freedom.

When you feel the urge to hang a "Do Not Disturb" sign over your heart, remember this: God already knows what's behind that door. He knows the anger, the grief, the exhaustion, and the thoughts you can't put into words.

He's not put off by your silence, and He's not offended by your struggle. He simply waits for you to let Him step in, because He knows that isolation may feel like a refuge for a while, but His presence is the only place where your soul will ever truly rest.

Reflection Questions:

1. What emotions or thoughts most often cause you to withdraw or shut down from others?

2. Who in your life has tried to reach out to you when you were distant? How did you respond?

3. What step can you take today to open your heart to God and, if possible, to someone else?

4. Write a letter to God, sharing the thoughts and feelings you've been holding back, no matter how raw they may be.

Day 18

I Don't Need Church

"And let us consider and give attentive, continuous care to watching over one another, studying how we may stir up (stimulate and incite) to love and helpful deeds and noble activities, not forsaking or neglecting to assemble together [as believers], as is the habit of some people, but admonishing (warning, urging, and encouraging) one another, and all the more faithfully as you see the day approaching."
Hebrews 10:24–25 (AMPC)

It's a familiar thought: "I don't need church to have a relationship with God." And on the surface, there's some truth in that. A real relationship with God starts in the heart, not in a building. It's personal. It's sacred. But it was never designed to be private. When we say, "I don't need church," we're not just dismissing a building; we're distancing ourselves from the body of Christ, from the community God designed to help us grow, heal, and endure.

Let's be honest: for many, this belief doesn't come from a place of pride, but pain. People have been hurt in church. Some have experienced hypocrisy, judgment, rejection, or even abuse of authority. Those wounds run deep, and they make us skeptical, guarded, even bitter. To protect ourselves, we pull away and convince ourselves we're better off doing this walk with God alone.

But shutting ourselves away from community because of past hurts is like refusing medicine just because the first doctor made a mistake. It's like deciding never to drive again because your first car broke down. The truth is that healing happens in the right community. Hope grows when we find a circle of sincere believers seeking God together. True strength, safety, and growth come through genuine fellowship.

Church was never about polished pews or preachers in perfect suits. It's about people; broken, imperfect people; walking the same narrow road, learning together, stumbling, and rising again, being changed by God's grace side by side. It is not a museum for the holy, but a hospital for the hurting. That includes you. That includes me.

Even if you cannot physically enter a sanctuary right now, you are never separated from the Church. Every time you pray with another believer, gather for Bible study, sing worship songs, or offer encouragement to someone in need, you are living out the Church. Wherever Christ is at the center, His presence is always there.

Imagine a leaf cut off from its branch. It may remain green for a few days, but eventually it withers and die. That is what happens when a believer tries to live this walk in isolation. We grow weaker. Our perspective shifts. Our spiritual gifts remain unused. And slowly, we drift from the very accountability, encouragement, and wisdom that keep us spiritually alive.

Scripture reminds us that we are "many parts, yet one body in Christ" (1 Corinthians 12:12–27). Every part has a purpose. Your voice, your presence, your testimony; they matter more than you may realize. When you withdraw, the body is missing something it needs, and you miss what the body was meant to pour into you.

There's a reason Hebrews calls us to assemble and encourage one another, especially as we see the Day of Christ's return drawing near. We were created to carry each other's burdens, to stir one another toward love and good works, to remind each other that God is still faithful. When you're weary, someone else's faith can steady you. When you stumble, someone's strength can help you rise. When you're discouraged, another's word of wisdom can bring light into your darkness.

The enemy knows this, which is why he works so hard to convince us we're better off alone. A disconnected believer is a vulnerable believer. Alone, we are easier to deceive, easier to tempt, and easier to discourage. But in the community, faith multiplies. Hope is contagious. And love; the kind that forgives, restores, and builds up; has room to grow.

Even Jesus, in His most sorrowful moment at Gethsemane, invited His disciples to watch and pray with Him. If the Son of God refused to face His darkest hour alone, why should we?

If you've been hurt by people in the church, acknowledge it before God. He is not asking you to pretend it didn't hurt. He is asking you not to let the pain become your prison. Forgiveness may not erase the wound, but it keeps the wound from defining your future. Don't throw away the beauty of true fellowship because of the failure of a few. God can lead you to the right connections, even here, even now, if you're willing to open your heart again.

The Church is not just where we go. It is who we are; together. And when we gather, even in the simplest ways, Christ Himself stands among us.

Reflection Questions:

1.   What experiences; good or bad; have shaped your view of "church"?

2.   Is there someone you can pray, study, or worship with regularly, even where you are now?

3.   What step can you take this week to be part of a community of believers, even in a small way?

4.   How would you encourage someone else who says, "I don't need church" based on what Scripture teaches?

Day 19

Work Unto The Lord

"Whatever may be your task, work at it heartily (from the soul), as [something done] for the Lord and not for men, knowing [with all certainty] that it is from the Lord [and not from men] that you will receive the inheritance which is your [real] reward. [The One Whom] you are actually serving [is] the Lord Christ (the Messiah)." Colossians 3:23–24 (AMPC)

There is a tension many feel in the routines of daily life, a tension that grows in the grind of everyday tasks. You might find yourself scrubbing pots in the kitchen, folding laundry, cleaning floors, or working hard in the heat, and it feels like no one notices or cares. The pay may be minimal, and the appreciation even less. The question creeps in: *"Why am I even doing this? What's the point?"*

But what if the point is not the job, the paycheck, or the recognition? What if the point is that every task; no matter how menial, hidden, or unappreciated; can become holy when you realize who you are truly working for?

You are not working for a boss, a company, or an organization. As a follower of Christ, your labor—right here, right now—is not wasted. It is a sacred offering to the Lord. Every task you complete, every service you give, every responsibility you fulfill becomes worship when it is done for Him.

This shift in perspective changes everything. When you see your work through the lens of God's Word, your attitude transforms. The task itself may not change, but your purpose does. Your effort becomes a testimony. Your consistency becomes a light. Your integrity, even when no one thanks you, becomes a reflection of Christ to those around you.

The world measures value by wages and applause, but God doesn't. In His Kingdom, the currency is faithfulness, diligence, and a willing heart. He is watching how you handle this season; not to judge, but to shape you. The patience being stretched in you, the discipline being formed in you, and the humility being deepened in you are preparing you for the life He is building beyond these walls.

Jesus said, "He who is faithful in a very little thing is faithful also in much" (Luke 16:10, AMPC). What you do with these "little things;" even a mop, even a tray, even an unseen shift; is proving what you will do when God places greater things in your hands.

The enemy of this mindset is bitterness. Bitterness whispers, "They don't deserve my effort. I'm just used to it. I'm forgotten here." But bitterness blinds you to the blessing. When you choose to honor God with your work, even when no one notices, you declare to Heaven and Hell alike: *"I trust God more than this situation. I work for Him, not for them."*

Ephesians 6:7–8 (AMPC) says, "Rendering service readily with goodwill, as to the Lord and not to men, knowing that for whatever good anyone does, he will receive his reward from the Lord, whether he is slave or free." Even when no earthly supervisor acknowledges your labor, Heaven does. Your work becomes a declaration: *"God, I honor You here. I trust You to reward what others overlook."*

And it's not just about getting through this season. It's about becoming someone who carries integrity into the next chapter. The habits you form, the character you build, and the discipline you develop in quiet, unseen moments will resonate when you step into new opportunities. Your family, future employer, and community will recognize the strength of the integrity you cultivated when no one else was watching.

So let this truth take root in your heart: Your labor is not in vain. Whether you are sweeping a hallway or studying a trade, you are not just filling time; you are sowing seeds for your future. Work with all your heart because you know who you're really serving. Christ is your Master. He is your Provider. And He is your Rewarder. His benefits never run out, and His promises do not fail.

Reflection Questions:

1. In what ways have I been working with the wrong attitude or motives?

2. What does it mean to me personally to "work unto the Lord"?

3. Are there areas of my work or service that I've been neglecting because I feel overlooked or underpaid?

4. How can I shift my mindset to see my job as an opportunity to glorify God?

5. What fruit (growth, character, skills) have I seen in myself through the work I've been doing?

Day 20

Dollar And Cents

"He who is faithful in a very little [thing] is faithful also in much…"
Luke 16:10a (AMPC)

Life's challenges can sometimes shrink your perspective until it feels like all that matters are small transactions, daily routines, or what you can gain in the moment. A few dollars can feel like a fortune. Everyday items can take on outsized value. Before long, true worth can start to feel defined by possessions, trades, or numbers in an account.

But God's economy doesn't operate on material measures. His standard of worth is not based on your resources but on your stewardship, your faithfulness, and the posture of your heart.

Whether you make seventeen cents an hour or volunteer without a dime of pay, your labor still carries weight when it's done as service to the Lord. Heaven watches the floor swept with excellence, the tray handed out with kindness, the supplies distributed with patience and humility. What the world overlooks, God counts.

The world says that money equals power and status. But in the Kingdom, it isn't about how much you have, but what you do with what God has placed in your hands. The question is not, "How much is in my account?" but "Am I trustworthy with what I've been given?" Are you thankful for the small? Are you wise when it feels like you barely have enough? Are you willing to share with someone who has less, even when you have little yourself?

Let's be honest; some of us—or people we know—have made choices driven by money or the love of it. Hustling, scheming, and chasing quick cash often lead down a difficult path. But now, there's a chance to let God reshape how we understand provision, value, and true wealth. Scripture reminds us, "The love of money is a root of all kinds of evil" (1 Timothy 6:10). It's not money itself that harms us, but when money controls us, destruction follows.

God isn't testing the size of your income. He's testing the shape of your heart. Will you honor Him with the little? Will you manage your cents with sense? Will you thank Him for what others would be grateful to have? Gratitude is a form of wealth. Stewardship is a form of success.

Jesus honored a poor widow who gave only two small coins; not because of the amount, but because it was everything she had. Heaven measures by faith, not figures. The question is not how much you can get, but how much you can be trusted with.

How you manage what is in your hands now; however little; prepares you for how God can trust you later. This is not just about finances; it's about discipline, integrity, and maturity. Those lessons learned now will not only shape your future outside these walls but will also echo into your calling, relationships, and opportunities later on.

True wealth begins inside. You can have an account full of currency and still be spiritually bankrupt. You can also be flat broke and yet walk in peace and purpose because your trust is anchored in God. Jesus said, "Seek (aim at and strive after) first of all His kingdom and His righteousness (His way of doing and being right), and then all these things taken together will be given you besides" (Matthew 6:33, AMPC). That includes what you need to live. That includes peace that money cannot buy.

Envy, comparison, and discontentment only chain your soul tighter. Don't measure your worth by what you own, or whose account is stacked, or who the richest person in the world is. You are not your balance, and respect is not for sale.

Today, I decided to shift from a survival mindset to a Kingdom mindset. Your dollars may be few, but when your heart is surrendered, even your cents carry eternal value.

Reflection Questions:

1. Have I placed too much worth on money or material things?

2. In what ways can I be more faithful with what I have, even if it feels small?

3. How does my attitude about work or money reveal my level of trust in God?

Day 21

The Betrayal Moment

"Even my own familiar friend, in whom I trusted, who ate my bread, has lifted up his heel against me." Psalm 41:9 (AMPC)

Betrayal always cuts close. It does not come from strangers or distant enemies, but from those who once sat at your table, shared your moments, heard your secrets, and held your trust. That is why it wounds so deeply, because it shatters the safety of the spaces you thought were sacred.

Many of us carry memories that still sting; a friend who turned informant, a partner who abandoned us, or a family member who spoke against us when we needed them most. The pain of betrayal lingers because it is more than an event; it feels like a tearing; a shattering that leaves our hearts raw and guarded.

Jesus understands this wound in full. Judas, who had walked with Him, eaten with Him, and witnessed His miracles, sold Him for thirty pieces of silver, and marked Him with a kiss. The disciples who swore loyalty scattered into the shadows when He was arrested. Jesus didn't just hear about betrayal, He felt it in the deepest, most personal way. He was not alone. Joseph was cast away by his own brothers and sold into slavery. David served Saul with loyalty, yet Saul hurled spears and plotted his death. Paul poured his life into churches, only to watch some turn cold and distant. The pages of Scripture show us that betrayal is not an end, but often the place where God begins something deeper.

God never wastes a betrayal. What others intend for harm, He bends toward growth and purpose. The moment someone turned against you may very well be the moment God began turning you toward Him, stripping away false alliances so you would lean on the One who never fails. The wound is real. There is no need to deny the pain or pretend it didn't cut you deeply. Betrayal is not something you simply "shake off." But the wound does not have to fester into bitterness. Betrayal does not have to become the prison of your heart. Healing begins the moment you allow God to touch that broken place and invite Him to release the weight of it.

Jesus still called Judas "friend" as he approached in the garden (Matthew 26:50). This was not weakness; it was strength rooted in the love and sovereignty of God. He forgave before the cross. He released the debt even as betrayal was still unfolding. God is not asking you to erase what happened, but He is asking you to release it, not for the betrayer's sake, but for your own freedom. Betrayal is not the end of your story. The enemy would have you believe that this wound defines your worth or derails your destiny, but Jesus proves the opposite. After the betrayal came the crucifixion, but after the crucifixion came resurrection. What was meant to destroy Him became the very path to His greatest victory.

When betrayal breaks your heart, let it build your discernment, deepen your dependence on God, and develop your capacity to forgive and love beyond what feels possible. It will reveal who truly stands with you, strip away illusions, and refine your trust, not in people first, but in God alone. And remember, you do not have to carry the burden of justice yourself. The Lord declares, "Vengeance is Mine, and recompense" (Romans 12:19, AMPC). You are free to lay down your need to clear your name or to even the score. God Himself will defend, heal, and vindicate you.

Sometimes, the very pain that feels like your undoing becomes the key to your deepest growth. Do not let betrayal harden your heart; let it press you closer to God, who never leaves or forsakes you. When others turned away, He turned His face toward you. His presence remains, His love is constant, and His purpose for you still stands.

Rise from the betrayal moment stronger, wiser, and more anchored in Him than ever before. Keep walking. On the other side of the wound, there is resurrection.

Reflection Questions:

1. Who has betrayed me, and how has it shaped the way I see others and God?

2. Am I still holding on to bitterness or anger, or have I chosen to release it?

3. What lessons is God teaching me about trust, discernment, and forgiveness through this betrayal?

Day 22

Don't Take It Personal

"Blessed (happy, to be envied, and spiritually prosperous, with life-joy and satisfaction in God's favor and salvation, regardless of their outward conditions) are you when people revile you and persecute you and say all kinds of evil things against you falsely on My account. Be glad and supremely joyful, for your reward in heaven is great (strong and intense); for in this same way people persecuted the prophets who were before you." Matthew 5:11–12 (AMPC)

There are few wounds deeper than being lied about, insulted, rejected, or treated as if your worth is invisible. When people turn their backs, twist your words, spread lies, or mistreat you, the first thought that echoes through your mind is often, *"What did I do wrong?"* That question can spiral into shame, anger, and self-doubt, threatening to rob you of peace and purpose. But there is a truth that silences that spiral: don't take it personally.

Not every wound you've endured is about *you*. Often, it's about the brokenness in others, their fears, insecurities, or even the spiritual battle raging inside them. And many times, the mistreatment you face isn't about *who you are*, but *Whose you are*. The enemy doesn't target the empty; he comes for the vessels filled with promise and purpose.

Jesus Himself shows us how to endure mistreatment without letting it poison our hearts. Beaten, mocked, spat on, and nailed to a cross, He did not internalize the cruelty or lash out in anger. Instead, He lifted His eyes to heaven and prayed, "Father, forgive them, for they know not what they do." That prayer wasn't weakness, it was unshakable strength, a grace rooted in knowing that His suffering was not meaningless but purposeful.

Some of the people who turned their backs on you, spoke against you, or hurt you may not truly understand who you are. They can't see your worth, can't handle your transformation, or can't comprehend the light God placed in you. Joseph's brothers didn't strip him of his coat simply because of the fabric;

they despised the calling it represented. Daniel wasn't thrown to lions because of wrongdoing, but because of his faithfulness. Jesus wasn't crucified because He failed, but because He fulfilled His assignment.

When insults, betrayal, or false accusations come, remember this: the attack is often confirmation. The enemy doesn't fire at empty targets. He strikes because there is something valuable inside you, something Heaven placed there that Hell wants to silence.

Yet, while you must not take it personally, you must also guard your heart from bitterness. Bitterness will chain you as tightly as rejection ever could. Guard your peace without hardening your spirit. Protect your heart without closing it off to grace. Show love and kindness where you can, not to invite abuse, but to rise above the dysfunction that tries to drag you down.

Sometimes, rejection is really God's redirection. Sometimes, betrayal is the bridge leading to your blessing. And the persecution you face may very well be proof that you are on the right path. Jesus reminds us that in Heaven's economy, every insult, every false accusation, and every rejection endured for His sake adds to a reward far greater than the pain.

So stand firm. Keep your eyes on Him. Let the offense grow you, not grind you down. Let it strengthen your faith, not scar your spirit. You were never meant to live for the applause of people. You were created to glorify God, and He sees every tear, hears every prayer, and promises that your reward will be greater than your suffering.

Walk in freedom. Forgive boldly. Love like Christ. And remember, it's not personal. It's purposeful.

Reflection Questions:

1. Who has hurt, insulted, or falsely accused me recently, and have I taken it too personally?

2. What truth from God's Word do I need to cling to when I'm rejected or misunderstood?

3. How can I protect my peace and guard my heart without losing compassion or closing off grace?

Day 23

Guarding Your Soul Against Agitation

"Do not let your hearts be troubled (distressed, agitated). You believe in and adhere to and trust in God; believe in and rely on Me also." John 14:1 (AMPC)

Life has a way of stirring unrest in the deepest parts of our being. The battles may be visible, chains, walls, and the weight of confinement, or invisible, rooted in memories, regret, fear, and uncertainty. Whether the prison is made of concrete or crafted within the mind, the enemy seizes every chance to disturb your peace. His goal is simple: to leave your soul agitated, restless, and distracted from the One who holds your future.

Yet Jesus speaks directly into the chaos: "Do not let your hearts be troubled." These are not empty words but a reminder that peace is a choice. Agitation will knock, storms will rage, and circumstances will provoke, but your heart doesn't have to bow to fear or unrest. Faith, not frustration, must govern your soul.

The enemy understands that a peaceful believer is a powerful believer. When your heart is calm, your ears are open to hear God. But when agitation sets in, your thoughts scatter, your emotions flare, and doubt begins to whisper louder than truth.

It doesn't always take much to unsettle us. A disrespectful word. A delayed response you were counting on. A memory from your past, heavy with regret or pain, creeping in like an uninvited guest. Before long, your spirit feels unsteady, and instead of walking in the Spirit, you are reacting from your flesh.

But remember: this war is deeper than people or situations. Ephesians 6:12 (AMPC) reminds us, "We are not wrestling with flesh and blood [contending only with physical opponents], but against the despotisms, against the powers, against [the master spirits who are] the world rulers of this present darkness, against the spirit forces of wickedness in the heavenly (supernatural) sphere." The real battle is for your peace, your focus, and your trust in God.

So how do you guard your heart when agitation tries to creep in? Not every situation that frustrates you is from God, and not every thought that enters your mind originates with Him either. The enemy will whisper lies, stir up misunderstandings, and provoke you toward reactions that derail your spiritual focus. When tension rises, pause and ask yourself:

Where is this agitation coming from? Is this thought or emotion from God, or is it the enemy trying to steal my peace? Am I about to react from my flesh, or can I stop and respond through the Spirit?

Jesus faced betrayal, lies, and relentless opposition, yet He moved with wisdom. He knew when to speak, when to stay silent, and when to retreat into prayer. He never let the schemes of the enemy dictate His response. Are you letting the enemy move you, or are you letting God guide you?

Psalm 119:165 (AMPC) reminds us, "Great peace have they who love Your law; nothing shall offend them or make them stumble." When your heart and mind are filled with God's Word, His truth acts as a shield, filtering out the triggers that lead to rash words or regretful actions. Instead of letting anger and anxiety take root, you anchor your emotions in the promises of God.

When anger rises, remember James 1:19 (AMPC): "Let every man be quick to hear [a ready listener], slow to speak, slow to take offense and to get angry." When anxiety presses in, hold fast to Philippians 4:6–7 (AMPC): "Do not fret or have any anxiety about anything, but in every circumstance and in everything, by prayer and petition (definite requests), with thanksgiving, continue to make your wants known to God. And God's peace [shall be yours…that] which transcends all understanding shall garrison and mount guard over your hearts and minds in Christ Jesus."

Each time you choose prayer over reaction, you rob the enemy of the foothold he seeks. Even a whispered prayer, "Lord, give me Your wisdom before I respond," can shift your spirit and silence the turmoil.

Sometimes, agitation lingers because we try to control what isn't ours to control, outcomes, justice, the timing of change. But peace doesn't come from control. It comes from surrender. Exodus 14:14 (AMPC) reminds us, "The Lord will fight for you, and you shall hold your peace and remain at rest."

Jesus left His disciples, and us, with this assurance in John 14:27 (AMPC): "Peace I leave with you; My [own] peace I now give and bequeath to you. Not as the world gives do I give to you. Do not let your hearts be troubled, neither let them be afraid." Your peace is not tied to the change of your situation, but to the unchanging presence of Christ. Even here, even now, you can refuse agitation and rest in Him.

Reflection Questions:

1. What situations or people tend to disturb my peace most often, and how can I approach them differently?

2. Am I spending enough time in God's Word so that His truth protects my mind and heart from agitation?

3. What areas of my life am I still trying to control instead of surrendering to God?

4. What burden am I carrying right now that God is inviting me to release?

5. Am I willing to trust Him fully with what I cannot change today?

Day 24

Honor Thy Temple

"Do you not know that your body is the temple (the very sanctuary) of the Holy Spirit Who lives within you, Whom you have received [as a Gift] from God? You are not your own. You were bought with a price [purchased with a preciousness and paid for, made His own]. So then, honor God and bring glory to Him in your body." 1 Corinthians 6:19–20 (AMPC)

There is a sacred truth that the world often buries beneath shame, rejection, and lies; a truth that many of us, especially those who have been told we are worthless, broken, or beyond repair, struggle to grasp. That truth is this: your body is a temple of the Holy Spirit. Even with the scars of your past, the choices you regret, or the wounds you still carry. God looks at you and calls your body sacred because His Spirit desires to dwell within you.

It's easy to neglect your body when life feels like it has neglected you. In challenging seasons, you might feel like your choices are limited or controlled by circumstances. Your schedule may be dictated by demands outside your control, and over time, it can be tempting to believe the lie that your body no longer matters—or worse, that you no longer matter. But Scripture tells us otherwise.

When you gave your life to Christ, you were purchased with a price; the precious blood of Jesus. That means you are not your own, not in the sense that you belong to a system, but because you belong to Him. You are not trash. You are not just flesh and bone. You are a vessel where the Spirit of the living God chooses to dwell.

Let that truth sink deep: the same God who crafted the stars, parted the seas, and breathed life into dust has chosen your body as His sanctuary. That means how you treat yourself, how you speak about your health, how you think about your identity and your worth; it all matters to Him.

To honor your temple means choosing not to engage with anything that harms your body, mind, or spirit—such as drugs, alcohol, abuse of prescription medications, violence, or unhealthy relationships. It means rejecting the harmful mindset of "I don't care what happens to me anymore." Honoring your temple isn't about being perfect; it's about showing reverence. It's about allowing God to cleanse what's been damaged, heal what's been broken, and restore what the world has labeled as lost.

Even within limited circumstances, there are ways to care for your temple. Drink water. Move your body when you can. Maintain hygiene. Rest when your body and mind need it. More than that, invite God into the process of healing what's beneath the surface; the soul wounds, the toxic thoughts, the identity struggles, and the shame that whispers lies about who you are.

Renewing your mind is just as vital as caring for your body. Romans 12:2 (AMPC) urges, "Do not be conformed to this world (this age), [fashioned after and adapted to its external, superficial customs], but be transformed (changed) by the [entire] renewal of your mind [by its new ideals and its new attitude]." Like we wash our bodies daily, our minds must be cleansed and renewed by God's truth. What we feed our thoughts through words, conversations, reading, and even self-talk; will either purify or pollute the temple.

Many of us grew up believing we weren't worth much. Some of us were used, neglected, or taught to weaponize our bodies for survival or self-defense. But when you came to Christ, He gave you a new identity. He calls you His. He calls your body a vessel of honor. When God sees you, He doesn't see wasted flesh; He sees a sanctuary that can reflect His glory.

This reverence extends beyond how we treat ourselves. When we degrade, threaten, or tear others down, we dishonor the living temples around us. We cannot shout praises on Sunday and curse our brothers and sisters on Monday without grieving the Spirit who dwells in us all. Our words carry power; they can either cleanse or contaminate the sanctuary God has chosen to dwell in.

And if you have dishonored your body in the past; through addiction, abuse, self-harm, or immorality; know this: God's grace is not exhausted. He offers healing that goes beyond the surface, sanctifying you spirit, soul, and body. 1 Thessalonians 5:23 (AMPC) declares, "May the God of peace Himself sanctify you through and through (separate you from profane things, make you pure and wholly consecrated to God); and may your spirit and soul and body be preserved sound and complete (and found blameless) at the coming of our Lord Jesus Christ."

You may carry scars; visible and invisible; but scars don't disqualify you. They are evidence that you survived, and in God's hands, they become testimonies of His power to redeem. You are not forsaken. You are not forgotten. You are scared. You are a temple where His glory still chooses to dwell.

The prison walls may confine you, but they cannot confine the Spirit of God living within you. Choose today to honor your temple; in your thoughts, your words, and your actions; and let the healing begin from the inside out.

Reflection Questions:

1. In what ways have I dishonored my body, through choices, thoughts, or actions?

2. What small, intentional steps can I take to begin honoring my body as God's temple, even here?

3. What lies about my worth, my identity or my body do I need to reject and replace with God's truth?

Day 25

It's Time To Unpack

Who are being guarded (garrisoned) by God's power through [your] faith [till you fully inherit that final] salvation that is ready to be revealed [for you] in the last time. I Peter 5:7 (AMPC)

Have you ever carried something for so long that you forgot just how heavy it was? Many of us didn't just arrive at a difficult place physically—we came weighed down by invisible chains. Chains of rejection, abandonment, shame, addiction, betrayal, anger, and unhealed grief. We arrived carrying more than what's visible; we brought years of emotional and spiritual burdens that have weighed heavily on us for decades.

And the truth is, many of us have worn that baggage so long that it feels like part of who we are. The hardness? It's not strength, it's a shield you built to survive. The anger? It's grief you never named. The silence? It's fear of being hurt again. What we often call "just my personality" is, in many cases, unprocessed pain that we've been dragging behind us for years.

But Christ calls you to more than survival. He calls you to lay down the weight you were never created to carry. He invites you to cast every anxiety, every wound, every scar, every secret onto Him, not because you have to be "fixed" first, but because He already carried it to the Cross. He does not shame you for your burden; He cares for you affectionately and watches over you with the intention to heal.

Unpacking that weight isn't weakness, it's courage. It's choosing to face the pain you've been avoiding, layer by layer, so you can finally heal. And it begins with honest surrender. Ask yourself: What am I still carrying that no longer serves my life or my future? Who am I still holding in unforgiveness? What lie about myself, or my worth have I been believing that God never said?

When we refuse to unpack, we carry our pain into every corner of our lives. We transfer it to our relationships, with cellmates, with friends, with family, and even with God. But Jesus doesn't ask you to fix yourself first. He simply says, "Come to Me." Unpacking begins with a choice:

Name the weight. Stop minimizing it. Call it out, abandonment, betrayal, rejection, abuse, regret. Bring it into the light through prayer, journaling, or confession to God. Release the lies. You are not your trauma. You are not your worst mistake. You are not beyond repair. God sees you not as you were, but as you are becoming.

Let God into the wound. He will not force His way into your pain, but if you open the door, He will begin to heal the places you've kept hidden. Psalm 34:18 reminds us, "The Lord is close to those who are of a broken heart and saves those who are crushed with sorrow in spirit."

Choose forgiveness. Not because the one who hurt you deserves it, but because *you* deserve freedom. Forgiveness is not agreement with what they did, it is the release that breaks their hold on your heart.

Fill the empty space with truth. Once you lay down the old, you must replace it with God's Word. Speak His promises over yourself daily, even when your environment contradicts it.

Some of us have been carrying pain and lies since childhood, weights we never asked for but learned to live under. But God is saying, *It's time to lay it down.* You can't build on a foundation full of clutter. You can't rise while dragging weights from the past. And God can't fill what you refuse to empty.

This may not be a quick process, but it will be a holy one. As you release the layers of trauma, guilt, shame, and anger, you'll begin to see the real you, not the labels others gave you, not the mask you wear to survive. But the beloved child of God, fully known, deeply loved, still chosen.

Your circumstances may feel confining, but they don't have to hold your soul captive. True freedom begins not when your situation changes, but when you let go of the burdens you were never meant to carry. It's time to unpack.

Reflection Questions:

1. What emotional or spiritual baggage have I been carrying that I've been too afraid to unpack?

2. How has holding onto these weights affected my relationships, my faith, and my ability to heal?

3. Am I willing to release my burdens to God so I can grow, even if the process feels painful at first?

Day 26

Not Today, Please

"Where no wise guidance is, the people fall, but in the multitude of counselors there is safety." Proverbs 11:14 (AMPC)

There are days when the weight you carry feels like too much. You don't want to talk. You don't want to see anyone. You're not angry at the world; you're just drained. Drained from pretending. Drained from pushing through. Drained from smiling while silently splintering into pieces no one can see.

So you shut down. A glance from someone feels like a threat. A kind question feels like an intrusion. You brush people off with, "I'm good," even when you're not. You're not trying to be rude; you just don't have the words to explain pain that you don't fully understand. Without saying it, your face and posture broadcast it loud and clear: "Please, don't bother me today."

That's what emotional shutdown feels like—the quiet closing of the heart, a silent sign hung over your soul that reads, "Out of Order." For many, this didn't start recently. It began long ago, in survival mode, when trauma taught you that being unseen was safer. It began when betrayal or disappointment whispered, "If you don't let anyone in, they can't hurt you again." Over time, isolation became not just a defense; it became a default.

But here's the truth: isolation may feel safe, but it's dangerous. It doesn't just shut people out; it slowly shuts God out too. Not in an instant, but over time. Prayer feels distant. Joy fades. You keep moving, but your soul stops living. Your heart goes numb, and numbness; though quieter than heartbreak, can be just as suffocating.

Proverbs 18:1 warns that isolation isn't neutral; it's destructive. When we retreat into ourselves, we not only seek our own way, but we rebel against wisdom, against perspective, against the very counsel that could help heal us. Alone, the enemy whispers lies more easily:

- "No one understands you."
- "People only show up when they want something."
- "You're better off alone."
- "Depend on no one; especially not God."

And without realizing it, those lies begin to sound like truth. They harden your heart, feeding the belief that silence is strength, when in reality, silence can strangle the soul.

Even Jesus, in His darkest hour, refused isolation. In Gethsemane, heavy with sorrow, He invited Peter, James, and John to watch and pray. He cried out to His Father, admitting His anguish, even saying, "If it is possible, let this cup pass from Me." Jesus didn't deny His pain, but He didn't shut down either. He let His soul be seen, and He stayed connected to His Father, even in agony.

You don't have to share every detail of your pain with everyone. But you can whisper a prayer. You can open your Bible, even if your hands feel heavy. You can answer when God nudges your heart and says, "Let Me in."

And maybe there's one person; a cellmate, a spouse, family member, co-worker, friend, or a chaplain; you can trust enough to say, "Today feels heavy. Will you pray for me?" That single moment of vulnerability can be the crack God uses to let light in.

Needing connection doesn't make you weak; it makes you human. God didn't create you to live locked in emotional exile, numb and withdrawn. He sees the heaviness you can't put into words. He knows the exhaustion you hide. And He's not put off by your silence, your mood, or your weariness. He simply asks for access.

So if today is one of those days when everything in you wants to hang the "Do Not Disturb" sign on your heart, let God be the one who gently knocks. Let Him soften what has hardened. Let Him sit with you in the silence and remind you: you are not alone, not forgotten, not forsaken.

Reflection Questions:

1. What signs show me that I've emotionally or spiritually shut down?

2. What situations or emotions usually trigger my need to isolate?

3. Have I been believing the lie that no one understands me? Where did that belief take root?

4. Can I write a letter to God, telling Him how I feel on my "Do Not Disturb" days, and invite Him into that space?

Day 27

From Time Into Eternity

"The Lord is near to those who are brokenhearted and saves such as are crushed with sorrow and humbled with regret." Psalm 34:18 (AMPC)

There are moments in life that stop everything, when the world keeps turning, but your heart feels frozen. Losing someone you love is one of those moments. The news hits like a freight train, and reality sinks in: you didn't get to say goodbye. You may never hold their hand again, kiss their forehead, or whisper "I love you" one more time. They've crossed from time into eternity... and you're still here. Grief is hard enough on its own, and sometimes it can feel almost unbearable.

There's no safe space to cry. No room to grieve privately. You might be in a noisy, crowded place or confined by your circumstances, surrounded by distractions while your soul is screaming in silence. It's one of the loneliest feelings in the world.

You may feel numb, confused, angry, or overwhelmed. You might find yourself going through the motions; but deep inside, you're broken. You try to hold it together because showing emotion in here feels like weakness. But hear me: grief is not weakness. It's love with nowhere to go. Even Jesus wept.

In John 11:35, the shortest verse in the Bible, we read: "Jesus wept." He wept at the tomb of Lazarus. Even though He knew resurrection was coming, He still felt the sting of death and the pain of loss. That tells us something powerful; God is not indifferent to our suffering. He enters it with us. You're not alone in this. God is with you.

Psalm 34:18 says, "The Lord is close to the brokenhearted and saves those who are crushed in spirit." That includes you. Whether your tears fall where no one can see them or your heart is too heavy to even cry, God sees. He knows. He cares. And He welcomes your grief.

You don't have to pretend with Him. You can be quiet in your own space and whisper, "Lord, I'm hurting." And He'll meet you right there—not with empty words, but with comfort and presence.

If your loved one knew the Lord, take heart; this goodbye is not forever. 1 Thessalonians 4:13 says we don't grieve as those who have no hope. For those in Christ, death is not the end. It's a doorway to eternal life. One day, you will be reunited in the presence of God, where there are no more tears, no more pain, and no more separation.

But what if they didn't know Jesus; or you're not sure? You can still trust them to the mercy of God. Only He sees the full picture. Only He knows what happened in the final moments. And His mercy runs deeper than we could ever imagine. Let that truth quiet your heart.

Still, grief has a way of dragging guilt into the room. You may be thinking: "I should've been there." "I didn't say what I needed to say." "I wasted too much time."

But guilt is not from God. That's shame trying to suffocate your healing. Conviction from God leads to repentance and life. Shame only brings bondage. If there are things you wish you had done differently, give them to God. Let Him redeem your regrets. Let Him teach you through them. But don't let them define you. You are still here. And you still have a purpose.

This loss doesn't mean your life is over. It means something inside you has changed; and God wants to walk with you through that change. He wants to take your grief and turn it into growth. He wants to show you how to live with loss but not be destroyed by it.

And what if you haven't experienced this kind of loss yet? Then you need to know how to walk alongside someone who has experienced loss.

If a friend just found out their mother passed… if a coworker is grieving her father… if someone nearby is sitting in silence, stunned and shattered by the news—be there. You don't need fancy words. You don't need to "fix it." You just need to show up.

Sit with them. Listen if they want to talk. Offer a tissue, a prayer, or just your quiet presence. Romans 12:15 says, "Rejoice with those who rejoice; mourn with those who mourn." In other words; be human. Be compassionate. Be like Christ.

Sometimes the most healing words are: "I'm so sorry." "I'm here for you." "I'm praying for your strength." Be the kind of person who brings peace, not pressure. Who brings comfort, not correction. Who shows love, not distance. We don't always know what to say when someone dies; but we can always show love.

And for you, the one grieving: take this season one day at a time. Let yourself feel. Don't rush healing. Write about your loved one. Talk to God about them. Ask Him to help you remember the good, release the pain, and carry their memory with honor, not shame.

They may be gone from time; but they've stepped into eternity. You're still here because God is not done with you yet. You are not alone. You are not forgotten. God is walking with you, from time into eternity.

Reflection Questions:

1. Who have I lost that left a lasting impact on my life? What do I miss most about them?

2. What emotions do I feel about their passing that I haven't expressed to God?

3. What regrets or guilt am I carrying? What truth does God speak to those feelings?

4. How can I honor their memory while continuing to live with purpose?

Day 28

Not Like Us

"Can a woman forget her nursing child, that she should not have compassion on the son of her womb? Yes, they may forget, yet I will not forget you. Behold, I have indelibly imprinted (tattooed a picture of) you on the palm of each of My hands..."
Isaiah 49:15–16 (AMPC)

There is something sacred and healing about realizing that God is not like us. He is not like the ones who raised us yet failed to protect us, the ones who abandoned us in our most vulnerable years, or those whose wounds spilled over and became our inheritance. He is not like the father who never showed up or the one who sat in silence as you tried to piece together your identity. He is not like the mother who may have loved you but didn't know how to nurture your soul, or the one whose pain screamed louder than her love. God is not like them.

You may have grown up without a father's embrace or a mother's affirmation. Maybe you never heard, "I'm proud of you," or "I love you," from the people who should have said it most. Without guidance, you sought identity wherever you could find it, on corners, in gangs, in relationships, or through sheer survival instinct.

What remains is a wound that few talk about but nearly all carry. Some call it the father wound; a deep, unhealed emptiness where unconditional love and affirmation should have been. For others, it is a mother wound; the ache of never being nurtured, seen, or valued. And often, these wounds echo into adulthood, fueling anger, mistrust, rebellion, or an endless search for worth.

This isn't about shaming your parents. Many of them were broken, too. It's about honesty because wounds you won't face will keep shaping your choices. When ignored, these wounds push us toward false identities, destructive cycles, and empty pursuits, trying to fill what only God can heal.

But here is the truth that changes everything: **God the Father is not like them.** His love is unlike human love; perfect, patient, and present. He is the Father your soul was created for. The One who knows your name, your story, and the exact number of hairs on your head (Luke 12:7, AMPC). He has never turned His face from you. Even in chaos, even when you couldn't feel Him, He was there.

To the brothers reading this: you don't need to keep hiding behind toughness or silent rage. Real strength is not found in burying your wounds but in letting God touch and heal them. It is okay to admit: "I needed more love. I was hurt when my father wasn't there." It is okay to let the walls down in the presence of the One who will never abandon you.

To the sisters: God sees the child in you who sought care but faced exploitation. He sees the woman who was discarded, used, or betrayed and now carries a heaviness few could bear. He has never used you. He has never rejected you. He calls you beloved, chosen, and worthy of His relentless love.

He understands it all; the child in you who just wanted to be seen and safe, the teenager who acted out because the pain felt louder than the silence, or the adult who is still piecing together a fractured sense of self. And to each of those parts of you, He says: "You are Mine. I have called you by name; you are not abandoned, not forgotten, not forsaken. I will never leave you nor fail you." (Hebrews 13:5 AMPC)

God's love isn't something you earn by performing or behaving. It's not based on how "good" or "obedient" you are; it flows out of who He is. He loved you on your worst day as much as He does on your best. When others walked away, He drew closer. When the world gave up on you, He still saw your purpose. When you felt silenced, He still heard every unspoken prayer.

And maybe, even if you let Him heal you, He will use you to help heal someone else. There is someone around you who is carrying the same wounds you know well. Maybe God has placed you there to be a brother, a sister, a reminder that not all love wounds; and that His love can heal every scar. Romans 12:15 says, "Rejoice with those who rejoice, weep with those who weep." Sometimes your listening ear, your quiet prayer, or your gentle presence is what opens the door to someone else's breakthrough.

God alone can re-parent your soul. He can teach you to receive the love you were denied and show you how to give what you never got. And in time, the very wounds that once broke you will become the testimony that brings healing to others.

You are not who they said you were. You are not what they failed to say. You are who God declares you to be; fully known, deeply loved, and forever His. And unlike every flawed human, He is and always will be God… not like us.

Reflection Questions:

1. Who do I still carry pain from; my father, my mother, or both? Have I been honest about how it shaped me?

2. How has this wound affected the way I see myself, others, and God?

3. What would forgiveness look like, not for their sake, but for my peace and freedom?

4. If I wrote a letter to God as my perfect Father, what would I tell Him that I never heard growing up?

5. Is there someone around me carrying a parent wound? How can I reflect God's comfort to them today?

Day 29

Gratitude During Darkness

"Thank [God] in everything [no matter what the circumstances may be, be thankful and give thanks]; for this is the will of God for you [who are] in Christ Jesus [the Revealer and Mediator of that will]." 1 Thessalonians 5:18 (AMPC)

Gratitude may feel like the furthest thing from your mind right now. When life feels stripped of joy, your freedom reduced to a memory, and every moment shaped by circumstances beyond your control, the thought of giving thanks can feel not only strange but almost offensive. You may even find yourself asking, *"What exactly am I supposed to be thankful for in a season like this?"*

The weight of hardship is heavy. It's not only the challenges you face, but also the isolation, the distance from loved ones, the milestones you missed, the guilt, the regret, and the gnawing ache of wondering how life ended up here. Gratitude, at first thought, sounds like something for people whose lives overflow with blessings—not for someone simply trying to make it through another day. And yet, gratitude may be the very thing your soul is starving for in this season.

Giving thanks does not mean pretending everything is okay when it isn't. It is not a denial of your pain or an invitation to fake a smile and suppress your emotions. Gratitude is not saying, *"I'm glad this happened"* or *"Everything's fine."* Sincere gratitude runs deeper than circumstance. It is not a reaction to perfection; it is a decision to trust. It is a deliberate declaration of faith—a choice to focus not on what has been taken, but on what God is still doing, even in the darkest places.

Bitterness, anger, hopelessness, and numbness come naturally in pain. But gratitude? That is supernatural. That is what lifts your eyes above the chaos and reminds your heart that the same God who created the stars has not abandoned you.

Perhaps you wonder, *"Why would God want me to be thankful in a time like this? Why would He ask that of me when everything feels like punishment?"* The answer is not that He wants you to be thankful **for** your pain. Rather, He calls you to be thankful **in** your pain. Gratitude doesn't mean you like where you are—it means you trust that where you are is not where your story ends. It keeps your heart open to see that God is still present, still working, and still weaving redemption even when nothing feels redemptive.

Paul, who wrote much of the New Testament, knew confinement and injustice firsthand. From a place of deep trial, he penned words that still echo through centuries: *"Thank God in everything."* Paul discovered something most of us never learn until everything is stripped away: God's presence is not confined by walls, distance, or the judgment of others. If Paul could worship in his darkest hour, maybe, just maybe, you can find a reason to thank God in yours.

If nothing comes to mind right now, take a slow breath and shift your focus. Gratitude often begins not with something big, but with something simple.

Maybe you can thank God that:
- You woke up this morning with another chance to live.
- You still have your right mind after everything you've endured.
- You survived what should have destroyed you.
- God continues to pursue you, even when others have turned away.
- There is still purpose in you, even if you cannot yet see it clearly.

These are not trivial things. They are evidence of grace.

Consider Paul and Silas in Acts 16. They were beaten, chained, and locked in the darkest part of a prison. No comfort. No rescue in sight. And yet, at midnight, the darkest hour of their trial, they prayed and sang praises to God—not because their circumstances were good, but because they trusted the One who is good. Their midnight praise shook the very foundations of the place they were in. Chains fell off. Doors opened. Their surroundings changed only after their hearts shifted.

Your situation may not change overnight. The walls around you may not crumble today. But when you choose to praise and thank God—even in your personal midnight hour—something will shift inside of you. Bitterness loosens its grip. Despair begins to crack. Hope takes root. The external may remain the same, but your spirit will rise.

Gratitude is more than a feeling; it is a weapon. It silences the enemy's whispers that you are forgotten, worthless, or beyond redemption. Gratitude speaks back

100

to despair and declares, *"God is still here. I still belong to Him. And this season will not define my eternity."*

Gratitude does four things:

- It sharpens your awareness of God's presence in your life.
- It begins with healing wounds you thought would never close.
- It softens your heart when bitterness tries to harden it.
- It strengthens your spirit to endure today so you can reach tomorrow.

You don't have to feel grateful to begin living with gratitude. Start small.

Whisper thanks before you complain. Take one breath before you react and ask God to show you one good thing in your day. It could be a kind word, a verse that lifts your spirit, a message that came right on time, or a fleeting moment of peace in your soul. Thank Him for that.

Gratitude does not deny the darkness; it ignites light within it. It's your heart choosing to say, *"God, I trust You—even here, even now. You are still good. And You are still worthy of my praise."*

Let thankfulness become your anchor. Let hope breathe life back into your soul. You are not forgotten. You are not finished. Gratitude is the doorway to hope and hope always leads to freedom—freedom of the heart, even before anything else changes.

Reflection Questions:

1. What is one thing I can thank God for right now, even if it feels small?

2. How does gratitude shift my thoughts and emotions, even when my situation does not change?

3. Have I ever felt peace or joy in a painful season? What did I learn in that moment?

4. Who is one person I am thankful for today, and how can I pray for them?

5. Can I write a short letter to God, expressing thanks, even if the words feel hard to find?

Day 30

Close the Door

"Thank [God] in everything [no matter what the circumstances may be, be thankful and give thanks]; for this is the will of God for you [who are] in Christ Jesus [the Revealer and Mediator of that will]." ; 1 Thessalonians 5:18 (AMPC)
"To everything there is a season, and a time for every matter or purpose under heaven." Ecclesiastes 3:1 (AMPC)

We are familiar with the natural rhythm of life, Spring, Summer, Fall, and Winter. These seasons shape how we live, how we prepare, and how we adjust. We do not fight their cycles because we understand they serve a purpose. But in the Kingdom of God, there is another kind of season that has nothing to do with weather or calendars. It is called Due Season.

Due Season is that divine moment when God whispers, "You have waited long enough. The time has come." It is when the seeds you planted through tears and perseverance begin to sprout. It is when growth, choked by toxic soil, negative voices, or the residue of past pain, finally breaks through. But here is the truth most do not want to face before Due Season can fully manifest, there must be a reckoning. An inventory. A holy evaluation of what and who surrounds you. And then, there must be courage to do what is hard but necessary, close the doors that no longer lead to life.

Closing doors does not mean hatred or bitterness. It does not erase the role someone played in your story or deny their value in a past season. It simply acknowledges a truth: not everyone and everything can go with you into where God is taking you next. Some relationships, habits, mindsets, and attachments were vital for your survival in one season but will sabotage your destiny in the next.

Think of the connections you are still holding onto out of guilt, nostalgia, or fear of loneliness. Ask yourself honestly: "Do they pour into me, or do they only pull from me? Are they helping me grow, or keeping me bound?" Some people attach themselves like leeches, appearing as friends but silently draining your vision, joy, and peace. And toxicity is not always a person; it can be a destructive habit, an unhealthy pattern, or a thought cycle that keeps you stuck.

Many of us keep trying to carry dead weight into the very spaces we begged God to open for us. But He is saying, "You cannot step into your Due Season dragging dysfunction God already told you to drop." Some connections brought more pain than healing, more confusion than clarity, more pain than power. Keeping them is to risk the very breakthrough you prayed for.

Even Jesus modeled this principle. He often withdrew from the crowds to be alone with the Father, guarding His focus. And in His closest circle, there was Judas, a man who had proximity to the table but no alignment with the mission. When Judas' time came, Jesus did not beg him to stay. He simply said, "What you are about to do, do quickly" (John 13:27). No drama. No bargaining. Just release. Why? Because even betrayal, when surrendered to God, becomes a bridge to destiny.

The truth is that some people will not be able to handle who you are becoming. They only recognize the broken version of you, the version who needed their approval, their dysfunction, or their validation. But when you begin to heal, grow, and rise, they must either rise with you or recoil from you. Both responses reveal the truth: growth often requires outgrowing.

Yes, some of these people were present in your darkest moments when you had nothing. But that does not mean they are equipped to stand with you in your becoming. Some were essential for your survival but cannot be part of your revival.

And here lies the tension: God is calling you to more. But "more" requires maturity, and maturity requires honesty. Honesty requires inventory.

Ask yourself with boldness:
- Who or what is draining my energy, vision, and faith?
- What cycles keep me circling the same wounds and pain?
- Who do I continue to forgive, yet never see fruit of real change?
- What patterns feed dysfunction and starve the purpose God planted in me?

You cannot heal what you will not face. And you cannot enter Due Season still chained to what God is trying to prune. Jesus said in John 15:2 that every fruitful branch is pruned, not punished, so it can produce more. Pruning feels painful, but it is purposeful.

Some doors remain open simply because you fear being alone. But hear this: solitude with God is safer than being surrounded by people who poison your soil. Separation is not always punishment; it is often protection. Silence, when surrendered to God, can be sacred. And in time, you will see why certain doors had to close.

You will look back and realize that what you thought you needed was actually a chain. That relationship, that mindset, that friendship, it was a lid on your life. It was not until the door closed that you could see the light, breathe again, and grow.

Due Season is a harvest season, but harvest requires separation. The wheat and the weeds grow together for a time, but the reaping must come. This is that moment. The season where God declares, "Enough. You have wept long enough. You have been bound long enough. Now, it is time to grow."

You are not wrong for craving peace. You are not selfish for setting boundaries. You are not cruel for choosing health over history. You are not heartless for walking away from what no longer serves your purpose. This is your Due Season. Your "no" is holy. Your silence is sacred. Your shift is necessary.

Do not leave doors cracked out of guilt. Do not chase those God told you to release. Do not apologize for healing. Do not apologize for changing. Let people say, "You're different." That is the goal. You were never meant to stay the same.

Love people, but from a distance if necessary. Pray for them, but without pulling them into your process. Forgive them, but without inviting them back into what God has set you apart for. Some doors must close so new ones can open.

Do not fear pruning. Embrace it. Because on the other side of obedience and release is your Due Season. Let today be the day you declare, "No more." No more settling. No more cycles. No more tolerating what refuses to grow.

You are not here to be tolerated, you were created to thrive, to bear fruit, and to step into the life God always intended. And sometimes, it begins with the courage to say: "This door must close so God's promise can open."

Reflection Questions:

1. What doors in my life has God been urging me to close, but I have left open out of fear, guilt, or habit?

2. Who or what consistently causes more harm than good in my journey, and why am I still holding on?

3. Am I willing to step into my Due Season, even if it requires me to walk alone for a time?

Day 31

Good Night, Lord

"Evening, and morning, and at noon will I utter my complaint and moan and sigh; and He will hear my voice." Psalm 55:17 (AMPC)

From the moment your eyes open to the moment they close, life moves at a pace that wears on both body and soul. Even in the midst of routine and pressure, days can feel overwhelming filled with noise, tension, swirling emotions, and spiritual fatigue pulling at every corner of your mind. Whether you're facing conflict, grieving the absence of loved ones, or simply trying to hold yourself together, one truth remains: God still wants to hear from you.

Prayer is not a ritual or a box to check; it is a lifeline. It is not reserved for Sunday services or emergencies, it is an invitation to commune with the One who never sleeps and never leaves. And perhaps one of the most overlooked yet powerful times to connect with Him is not at dawn or mid-morning, but when the day winds down, when you whisper before you close your eyes: **"Good night, Lord."**

Psalm 55:17 reminds us that prayer is not confined to a moment but is a rhythm, *evening, morning, and noon*. It reflects a life open to God's presence throughout every season of the day. He listens when you get it right, but also when you stumble, when your faith feels faint, and when your heart feels too heavy to find the words.

Ending your day in prayer is not just about habit, it is about finding **refuge**. For some, night brings quiet and calm; for others, it ushers in the loudest battles. Memories return. Regret becomes sharper. Fear or grief creeps in when the world slows down. But when you choose to end your day with God, everything shifts. Your bunk becomes more than a bed; it becomes an altar. Your tears become a hymn. The darkness becomes a sanctuary where His light can meet you. And you can lay the day before Him and say, "Father, I release it all back to You."

Psalm 62:8 says: "Trust in, lean on, rely on, and have confidence in Him at all times, you people; pour out your hearts before Him. God is a refuge for us." (AMPC) That includes the quiet hours when your thoughts feel loudest. You do not have to fall asleep suffocating beneath the weight of what you carried all day. You can pour it out, sigh by sigh, tear by tear, word by word, and find rest.

Tell Him what hurt today. Thank Him for what you survived. Confess what you regret. Ask Him for strength to forgive. Release the frustration, the fears, the questions, and the burdens you were never designed to carry.

And then be still. Breathe. Let His peace cover the chaos. Let His presence quiet the racing of your mind. The same God who spoke peace to a raging sea can speak peace to the storm inside of you tonight.

Nights can feel suffocating. The lights dim, the noise fades, yet inside, the battle in your mind intensifies. But even in the stillness and quiet, the Father bends His ear to your voice. Psalm 4:8 declares: "In peace I will both lie down and sleep, for You, Lord, alone make me dwell in safety and confident trust." (AMPC). This is more than poetry; it is a promise. You can lie down in peace, not because your surroundings are ideal, but because your Savior is present. His nearness, not the absence of problems, is what allows you to truly rest.

Ending your day with prayer also creates space for reflection. These quiet conversations with God allow you to trace His fingerprints through your day, to recognize the moments He protected you, corrected you, encouraged you, or simply kept you standing when you felt weak. Reflection stirs gratitude, strengthens faith, and roots your emotions in the unshakable truth that God is near. Even Jesus modeled this. Luke 5:16 says, *"But He Himself withdrew [in retirement] to the wilderness (desert) and prayed."* (AMPC) The Savior of the world, who carried the weight of humanity, still made time to withdraw and commune with His Father. If He needed these moments, how much more do we?

Gratitude, especially at the end of a long day, has the power to shift the atmosphere of your heart. It does not deny pain, but it invites God's presence into it. 1 Thessalonians 5:18 (AMPC) tells us: *"Thank [God] in everything [no matter what the circumstances may be, be thankful and give thanks]; for this is the will of God for you [who are] in Christ Jesus [the Revealer and Mediator of that will]."*

It does not say to thank Him **for** everything, but to thank Him **in** everything. Even in the darkest nights of the soul, you can still find gratitude to thank Him for, breath, strength, life, protection, provisions, and His Presence in your life. Gratitude loosens the grip of despair and brings warmth and hope into the coldest corners of your circumstances.

And as you close your day, speak peace, and hope over tomorrow. Declare God's Word as a covering over your rest and your future:

- "The Lord will perfect that which concerns me." (Psalm 138:8, AMPC)
- "And I am convinced and sure of this very thing, that He Who began a good work in you will continue until the day of Jesus Christ, developing, perfecting, and bringing it to full completion." (Philippians 1:6, AMPC)
- "Surely goodness and mercy *and* unfailing love shall follow me all the days of my life, and I shall dwell forever [throughout all my days] in the house *and* in the presence of the Lord." (Psalm 23:6 AMP)

You are not forgotten. You are not abandoned. Your night is not the end of your story; it is simply the pause before a new chapter begins. So when the lights dim and your body begins to rest, don't let your mind spiral into darkness. Don't let despair take the final word. Instead, whisper a prayer that carries eternal weight:

"Good night, Lord. I trust You with what I cannot change. I release what I cannot carry. I rest because You do not sleep. I thank You for today, even the hard parts. I lay down my burdens and my breath in Your hands. Good night, Lord."

Reflection Questions:

1. What part of today am I most grateful for?

2. Is there anything I need to confess, release, or forgive before I rest?

3. Where did I sense God's nearness or protection today?

4. Which scripture can I speak over myself as I prepare for tomorrow?

Locked In But Not Locked Out

About The Author

Albert J. Yancey III discovered the depth of his purpose in a place he least expected, behind prison walls. His powerful devotional, Locked In But Not Locked Out, was born from a transformative journey marked by pain, process, and, ultimately, divine purpose.

Raised in an underserved community, Albert faced many challenges familiar to countless young men: fatherlessness, inner turmoil, negative influences, and an overwhelming hunger for identity and belonging. The choices he made in search of these things led him down a path that ended in incarceration. Yet, it was within the confinement of a prison cell; designed to break him; that he found healing through God's grace.

In that cell, Albert encountered more than mere religion; he found a profound, personal relationship with a God who redeems and restores. Immersing himself in Scripture, daily writing, fervent prayer, and intentional reflection, he experienced genuine transformation. Albert became an encourager, offering hope and compassion to others who were hurting, confused, or forgotten; knowing their pain intimately because it mirrored his own.

Upon his release, Albert founded Faith Beyond Incarceration (FBI) Ministry, a 501(c)(3) nonprofit organization dedicated to reducing recidivism and promoting public safety. FBI Ministry equips individuals impacted by the justice system with essential resources such as housing, employment opportunities, mental health support, education, and spiritual mentorship.

Today, Faith Beyond Incarceration has grown into a movement centered around healing, restoration, and advocacy, driven by the belief that no individual is beyond reach and no story too broken for God to use.

Albert wrote this devotional specifically for incarcerated souls, but its reach extends far beyond physical prison walls. It speaks to anyone feeling locked in, whether trapped in emotional turmoil, spiritual stagnation, mental confusion, or destructive cycles. Recognizing that prisons come in many forms, this devotional serves as a key, offering readers liberation not only from confinement but also from the bondage of the heart.

Each devotional entry is crafted with intention, honesty, and hope, designed to ignite a hunger for purpose, a deeper trust in God, and an unwavering resolve to persevere.

Albert's life testifies to a powerful truth: Though you may feel locked in, you are never locked out of God's grace, mercy, or His purpose for your life.

In grace and truth,

Albert J. Yancey III
Founder
Faith Beyond Incarceration Ministry (FBI)
www.fbiministry.org

www.ingramcontent.com/pod-product-compliance
Lightning Source LLC
Chambersburg PA
CBHW060633130626
46555CB00002B/780